Polishing the Fragments

John Kaniecki

Polishing the Fragments
Copyright © 2017 by John Kaniecki

Disclaimer: Some names and identifying details have been changed to protect the privacy of individuals. The author has tried to recreate events, locales and conversations from his memories of them. None of the information in this book is intended as medical or psychological advice, nor is any information in this book meant for any purpose other than for the author to tell his personal story. The publisher and author assume no liability for any damage or disruption caused by the contents of this book.

Cover Art
Macario Hernandez III
Editors
Blair Hill
Sarah White
Editor-in-Chief
Kristi King-Morgan
Formatting
Niki Browning

All rights reserved. This book or any portion thereof may not be reproduced or used in any manner whatsoever without the express written permission of the publisher except for the use of brief quotations in a book review.

Printed in the United States of America

First Printing, 2016

ISBN 13: 978-1-947381-03-2
ISBN 10: 1-947381-03-2
Dreaming Big Publications

www.dreamingbigpublications.com

This book is dedicated to my beautiful wife Sylvia Kaniecki.

Contents

Mother's Madness 7
Waiting For The Shrink 9
Doctor Rodney Matz 10
My First Psychiatrist 12
At The New York Aquarium 14
Raised By A Broken Man 15
Power Of Poetry 16
The Song Of Life 18
Passion Of The Born-Again Poet 20
Yes I Care 21
Pictures 23
Stolen Water 25
Moments In Late Night 26
Walter Is Dead 28
Crash And Burn 30
Dreams 32
When Marianne Ran Away 33
Sleepless Night 35
In The Greater Epic 36
Almost The Word Of God 38
Mother In The Nursing Home 40
Nature Or Nurture 42
On The Road 43
Youth 44
My Mirror 45
In The Context 46
So Much, So Little 48
I Hear Your Voice 49
Depraved Hatred Of Dutch Demons 51
Petition To Ban Nuclear Weapons 52
Into The Future 54
Super Intelligent Fools 56

Stigma	58
Coming Of The Storm	60
The Least Of These	62
Indie Book Fair	64
On The Mountain Top With A Dirty Sky	66
Pumpkin Head Peter	68
First Time In A Committed Psychiatric Ward	70
Picture Perfection	72
Loose Wire	74
An Interlude	76
The Great Beyond	78
Haunting Dreams	80
A Poet's Pain	82
The Great Critic	84
Driving Dementia	86
Our Garden	88
You Sing The Blues	90
Peace Action	92
Hallelujah	94
The Sin Of Poverty	96
Whitey's On The Moon	98
Satan's ABC's	100
The Lesser Of Two Evils	102
Words	104
The Perfect Ten	106
The Twist	108
A World Of Giving	110
A Lecture In Life	112
A Long Night	114
Rock And Roll And Rock	116
The Heart Of The Artist	118
Red Blue Green And Of Course Invisible	120
Time	122
Working Hard	124
Stress	126
Death And After Life	128
A Flash	130
My Eulogy	132

Mother's Madness

YOU GODDAMN SON OF A BITCH!!!
Sorry to awaken you
To have shaken you
To my reality
You Goddamn son of a bitch
It isn't even nice in a whisper is it?
I'm sure there were other words
She sure as hell yelled enough

One day
Walter and I were playing, a game called Clue
We were too young to understand the rules
Mother was screaming
SCREAMING, SCREAMING, SCREAMING
Father came home
Red-faced in a rage
He could hear mother from up the block.
Father began to choke mother
In the corner where the Christmas Tree was always set up
A technique he must have learned in "Basic Training"
She squealed in anguished pain and terror
Marianne several years older
Began to pound Father on the back with her tiny fist
"YOU CAN KILL HER! YOU CAN KILL HER!!"
Walter and I were weeping
A lament to innocence lost
Father relented and stormed away

Years later
Father and I were discussing things of a religious nature
Most likely I was trying to convert him
"I have never sinned"
Was his bold profession
I asked him
"What about the time you choked mother?"
I cannot recall his facial expression
"Oh I apologized for that" was his flippant defense
There is no helping some people

John Kaniecki

I lost Sugar Mountain early
It blew up in a Volcano

Waiting For The Shrink

The wait is always long
I bring along my Bible
And of course my notebook and pen
Never know when inspiration
Will kiss you never to be seen again

He is a good psychiatrist
The visits are brief
Unless we talk politics of course
Perhaps I am a pleasant relief

Sometimes I have an issue or two
Sylvia my wife has dementia
My manic depression a blessing
As I peer intimately into her world
We have carried similar crosses

I hear voices
Pleasant and sweet
Wonderful voices
That make life complete
The shrink tolerates my condition
As long as I take my medicine
I stay out of hospitals

But apparently he is a busy, busy man
The waiting room is crowded
Nobody is smiling
Sometimes we will chat
There is the constant babysitter
That is the television
The Psalms are very soothing
David didn't have an easy life
And he was a king
Oh the joys and blessings
That waiting for the shrink brings

John Kaniecki

Doctor Rodney Matz

I was administered the Rorschach Test
By one Doctor Rodney Matz
He called in a nameless, ambiguous colleague to assist
In addition I was shown a picture
And told to create a story
Which I did
I always enjoyed fantasy
Thus my propensity now towards writing
I told them what these black splotches looked like
Mostly butterfly after butterfly in all honesty
But I don't think I dared to venture the path of simplicity
After all my sanity was on the line
My story I recall
Was a grand tale of meeting a stranger
Or perhaps waiting for a stranger
The diagnosis
After a humongous bill
Was that I was in need of treatment
By one Doctor Rodney Matz

Years of contemplation
The arrow on the compass always points North
It is my honest conclusion
That like a Vegas Slot Machine
In the long run the house always wins
There are no right answers
Only wrong ones
If it were otherwise
I would not have been recommended treatments
And my parents charged
Extravagant bills
By one Doctor Rodney Matz

So I found a new Moses to lead me to
The Promised Land of Sanity
By one Doctor Rodney Matz
Whose license would later be revoked
By the State of New Jersey

For professional misconduct
As he admitted sexual contact
With his psychiatric Patient E.J.
All I wanted to do was save the world
You tell me which one of us was sick

John Kaniecki

My First Psychiatrist

This nameless entity
Whom I would call Satan
But I fear to besmirch the devil
And make The Prince Of Evil look bad
Ah the poetic technique of hyperbole
The sheer terror of being committed
Constant observation
Thorazine cocktails
Horse tranquilizers for the uninitiated
Dancing as Zombies, laughing as perfect fools
Group therapy – confess your sins
Divulge your innermost fears
In front of complete strangers
As some Psych Tech observes
Jotting notes, scribbling in secretive code
Carnal curses of confusion
Ah and the visits from the god
The man who can release you
The man who can change your horrendous pills
The man who holds your eternal fate
The psychiatrist
"How are you doing today John?"
I attempt to shake his hand
Rudely he denies my overture
"Can I get out today" is my plea of desperation
"Not yet John"
It is a daily ritual of drudgery
There is no counseling
No exploration of my mental illness
Only an ominous thirty seconds
Simultaneously too short and too long
Upon release he shakes my hand
Has he lowered himself?
Or have I been elevated to the sanctity of the sane?
His bill is a down payment on a Mercedes
I refuse to see him further
There is no point
Thus I take an ill-informed step

Polishing the Fragments

To begin my psychological journey
On the thin icy edge of my torturous existence

John Kaniecki

At The New York Aquarium

I don't want you to think ill of mother
I love her dearly
As she did me
I point the blame to Father
Mother spent terrible trying years
Wondering what she did wrong
Until the realization
The greater sin was committed by her mate
There was the day at the Aquarium
Shining brighter than a perfect sunny day
Mother took us into New York City
Perhaps Walter was present
Sometimes life is hazy
All I remember was the fish
Tank after tank after tank
Beautiful, wondrous, magical
Colors, curiosities, comical creations
The shark cage was outstanding
White skinned, tall finned, long teeth snarling
Floating in a foreign world inches away
But I was too short to see anything!
So at every single exhibit
Mother took me in her arms and lifted me up
"I wanna see, I wanna see"
Into the cradle of her loving limbs
"I wanna see, I wanna see"
A hundred desperate pleas
Answered satisfactorily each time

Later mother would hostilely fight
With apathetic customer service agents
For the release of blood tests
So the pharmacy could relinquish my medicine
More ferocious than the great white sharks
Circling in intensity
At the New York Aquarium

Raised By A Broken Man

I was broken before I was formed
Smashed in the kiln
A flower
Plucked as a sprout
But life goes on
Soldiers constantly march to war
Like father
A double curse
Grandfather dying and being drafted
So he could liberate the Korean Peninsula
Never mind his personal dreams
Duty called dripping in its mockery
And all vestiges of his humanity perished
Wounded, scars never to heal
I pity the man
Scientist, soldier, intellect
Put food on the table and clothes on my back
Child of the depression
But no tender love
A hole inside a hole, black on black
His arrogance immense
PhD where the "P" stands for pompous
So many episodes of cold-heartedness
At his own mother's funeral
We are leaving the gravesite
The entire family in somber silence
Tears swelling in dad's eyes
I come near to embrace him
He harshly pushes me away
He thrusts his hand into a fist trying to be strong
I recall
"Jesus wept"

John Kaniecki

POWER OF POETRY

Poetic professions precisely pronounced
An intense archeological dig
The Ming Dynasty vase
More precious than pirates' hidden treasure
And of grander pleasure
Extracted word by word
From the dust Adam formed
Via the rib, thus came Eve
Ah but only if you believe
Creativity is from the Creator
A latent gift lurking in our subconscious
Therapy, relief, a work of art, pleasure in producing
Subliminal tremors permeating
My muse guides my pen
Adam Smith's invisible hand
A misery's merchants might understand

In a distant world in the back room of a University
Scholars with delicate care recreate
What was once an extraordinary vessel
Useful and above all beautiful
It held the radiant red roses
By which you were blessed
By which I professed
Undying love to you
Those were the good old days when you made the sky blue

CRASHING, SMASHING, BASHING

So here I sit in a display
Gawking curious tourists
Alienated by the glass case
Boldly declaring delicacy
Not to be touched
Only observed
Ah poems of sweet romance
But I cannot sing
But I cannot dance

Polishing the Fragments

I cannot do anything
Except perhaps converse
Such is my curse
The Ming Vase in the bulletproof prison
So elegant in appearance
But it cannot hold water

The Song Of Life

All the orchestra in their fine Tuxedos
Chains of gold binding them to their seats
Enter stage left an electric guitarist
The rocker is dressed in ripped blue jeans
Laying down a revolutionary rift
The cruel conductor fiercely frowns
But this is the song of life
I defy predestination embracing free choice
For ye see I know I have a voice
And I am speaking even now
So many sit politely at their meager piano
With simplistic sheet music before them
Do, Re, Me they tap the keyboard with a single finger
Twinkle, Twinkle Little Star
I soar in the heavens upon eagle's wings
Still I know my place
Blessings are all by grace
Perception is more than looking with your eyes
Vision is discerning past the lies
To dare to defy
To be bold and ask "Why?"
There is more to a song than the melody
The lyrics are truly the key
Words define, bind, create thoughts in the mind
Concepts and theories gather like clouds of rain
Truth came to me in a devastating deluge
You can sing however you please
You are free
You can sing however you please
But there are consequences to be had
Life thrust me down upon my knees
When I defied the god of Mammon
A psychiatrist came to examine
The diagnosis was that I was mad
Perhaps I was truly insane
But what of those clearly living life in vain
Corporations which destroy the environment
The military that violates young people's will

Polishing the Fragments

Creating automatons who willingly kill
Bankers who lustfully covet in zealous greed
Yet have more than they will ever need
And me, alas poor pitiful me
All I wanted to do was save humanity
But I sung out of key

John Kaniecki

Passion Of The Born-Again Poet

Poverty of the heart
A beating bankrupt mechanical machine
Void of the thrill of exhilarating art
Pumping the essence of mere meager existence
Always giving but never truly living
Until Love as a grand mystical force
Became the source
Born-again torn when I came to discover
That life itself was my sensual lover
To capture the universe in radical rhythmic verse
I kissed the desire
Embraced the fire
My blessing synonymous to the ultimate curse
I wondered in deepest compassion
The plight of the poor
The wickedness of war
I sought to define my place in time and space
In capturing the muse I was caught
In liberation and liberating I was taught
All the answers seemed to fade into the wind
And I guilty of the greatest sin
Convicted of looking with a blind eye
And being deaf to the overwhelming cry
It was change or die
To embrace the truth and forsake the lie
The hammer had struck
Fragments flew in diverse directions
Miserable woes, too numerous to mention
But the solace of my manic misery
Was the undeniable truth
I was free
They may give me a barbed wire crown
And crucify me in the darkness on the edge of town
Still I have the answer that the prophets sought
And life now full of the
Passion Of The Born-Again Poet
Would never again be for naught

Yes I Care

Green moons line dancing with purple stars
An army of angels armed with electric Stratocaster guitars
An expression that is the rarest of the rare
Yes I care
When I ask "How are you doing?"
I want to hear an honest report
Broken bones seared in sarcastic tones
So many scars each one crushing with a memory
Only in forgiveness are we fully free
If nothing else, I have a listening ear
Scarlet letters of primeval poetic prose
I dared to share what was precious beyond compare
My soul
Where was the love?
I was a hideous monster labeled as "insane"
Relegated to being hated
Beauty and the beast the greatest is the least
When all that you have is a prayer
Then you become aware
Yes I care
The beating heart thumping the intoxicated blood of the bum
Conquerors are overcome
Wall Street executives shuffling in sin
Coming down on coke snorting heroin
Still I'll let them in
For you see the equality of humanity
Self is always of primary importance
Loving is always a chance
Take a loss
The way of the cross
Giving relief to the remorseful thief
Such is my belief
Yes I care
I embraced the disgraced
I recall after all I was one of their number
Legions of psychotic searchers
Chased from churches

John Kaniecki

    Forbidden from dining in domains of dignity
    I have chased you from dream to nightmare
    Wherever I turn you are there
    Yes I care

Pictures

Snapshots of evidence
In the black and white photographs
In particular the one of Marianne, Walter and I
Smiles as we gleefully clutch presents under the Christmas tree
Was that truly us? I ask in shock
A time relegated to my far distant youth
Barren from my memory
Happiness was water in the sweltering desert, never a chance of rain
The genuine joy never to return
Rather smiles of forced concern
Mother never felt loved, nor did the children
Her anger antagonized by neglect
And massive lack of respect
As father had his Sunday golf outings
So much for the two becoming one
Or even little moments of fun
There was always work, watching football games and selfish pursuits
I understand from conversations much later down the line
That mother wanted to be a lawyer
And father never lived up to his promised obligations
Perhaps the toils of the family life were too numerous
Or it was brutal Brutus betrayal
I recall the seething fights
"You think you're so smart," hissed mother in toxic venom
In his arrogance father must have agreed
I recall Thanksgiving dinner
As at the dinner table he lectured my wife Sylvia about Grenada
Between bites of turkey he delivered his discourse
The pompous fool watched an hour show on public television
While Sylvia lived in that tropical paradise
Can you picture the scene?
I recall father in the hospital room
The diagnosis was that the stomach cancer was untreatable

John Kaniecki

> He could no longer eat or even defecate
> He was given two weeks to live
> "Perhaps you should start to consider God," I offered softly
> In a disgusting anger his response echoed pompously
> "I'm too busy trying to figure out a way to live"
> His withered arm wagging in anger
> "Fools go where angels fear to tread"
> We buried Father
> Not a solitary friend of his came to mourn, he had none
> A picture of an empty void
> Reminiscent of his heart

Stolen Water

Sylvia
Dementia rotting her brain
Bowling, how she loved to knock down pins
Tears roll down my cheek
Like the ball down the alley
"Sylvia, bowl the ball"
The faint vacant look of confusion
She retrieves the orange ball
"Here?" she asks
My heart snaps as I nod
It's the same place for the first four games
Once my lovely bride was a crystal blue river
Carrying the boat of our marriage
Merrily, Merrily, Merrily
We were sailing in good times
A pleasant breeze pleased
But now the water is toxic
The vibrant fish rot on the water's surface, all life has vanished
I dare not touch what once nourished me
What was the substance of my existence
Is now cursed anathema
Sylvia goes to bowl down the wrong lane
I scream in alarm
"No Sylvia, NO!!"
As if the world is ending in fire and brimstone
She is caught in this dark maze
Bumping into the wall over and over
Never knowing the reality
She simply has to open the door
And walk out to freedom
I wonder about the cruelty of God
As I pray for His tender mercy
But who am I to question the Almighty?
I thank Him for what I had
What I once loved before
Stolen water

John Kaniecki

Moments In Late Night

Death
Liberator or Tyrant?
The Shade has stolen mother, father
And sadly and prematurely
Walter was plucked from this life
Let me not philosophize
Rather open your precious eyes
What ferments in my mind
Is what I will leave behind
And so life is rich in meaning
And the Love is streaming
To live to give
So others down the line
May be blessed
To end all war
That none are bitterly poor
That the Earth is not raped

None of the guilty escaped
For though they mock human tribunals
Death shall not fail
And thus righteousness shall prevail
In the context of the betterment of all
I sit here typing, answering the higher call
Every time I walk by the barbed wire fence
I fume in highest offense
I give it a slight kick
This evil barrier that separates and divides
Behind which villains hide
Over the course of my existence
Thousands of times I attack the construction
Hoping it will fall
Perhaps it is vanity
But I am doing all that I can
And that makes me a man
If by chance these words shall die obscure
I can do no more
I fight this late night silent war

Polishing the Fragments

Contemplating poems for the higher good
Perhaps I shall be misunderstood
Blasphemed and deplored
But truly that is better
Than simply being ignored

Walter Is Dead

He wasn't a good brother
A dysfunctional family fosters agony
Not to say we never had our good times
Moments of play
But never a connection
Not even a slight one to mention
Arrogant as father
Despite lacking any worldly credentials
Angry, raging against the machine
As years rolled on by
He couldn't learn to let the past simply die
To take courage and understand that the torment and pain
That his dark deluge of rain
Could be something to motivate
Rather he simmered in tempestuous hate
Never learning the lesson of Love
Until God pricked him from above
And Walter learned his dreadful fate
That the cancer was found too late
Oh he put on a brave face
And manifested a commendable serving of grace
Gone was the mocking tongue
The rudeness, that my presence was an intrusion
Sadness resonates inside of me
Thinking how things should be
That brothers should have the deepest bond
Especially him being the elder
Somebody to look out for me
Rather I was cast away
Unwanted and useless
But when he was near the end
Things began to mend
I never told him I loved him
Certainly he never spoke those words to me
My Christian family urged adamantly
Let those words be said
Find the peace
Find the release

Polishing the Fragments

I was determined but the time was too short
So let me say in report
To Walter who failed this test
My last words were
"You can only do your best"

Crash And Burn

Compassion creating sympathy
Torturous torment of the test
We are all slave to some greater agony
Life is a raging battle
I cannot escape humanity's carnal curse
Pleasures of the flesh pressing perverse
Whispering seductive sensual secrets
David lusting Bathsheba's buxom beauty
We were born to fail
Do not count our attempts as vanity
Life's meaning is within the journey
How I need you and you need me
There is an equal inequality
No matter whom you may be
We are interrelated, connected
Parasites consume delicate delights
Some have no rights
Injustice hisses delivering her most wicked kisses
I cannot stand more of this
Then I turn
I learn
To give another try
Why?
It is the only answer I can render
Never surrender
Though you crash and burn
From the ashes
Learn
Try
If you forsake all hope
If you cannot cope
If you cannot rise from the misery of your bed
If dark demons molest every moment in your head
If plans of suicide dominate your every thought
If helpless at the bottom of the pit you are caught
If the night is cloudy and the moon eclipsed
Be aware
I've been there

To you this is my prayer
If you are crushed by the cross
Take it not as a loss
In time and space with God's grace
Once more you shall fly

Dreams

A haunting twisting melody
Murky misery mixing
An eternal fight to be free
Most never knowing love is the key
It will release your chains
And doubly inflict your pains
Dreams
Strange how they change and rearrange
As we achieve
All we believe
Become treasures of gold
What is the use?
Something pretty to wear
An earring dangling under your hair
Dreams
Be wise
Don't listen to the lies
As they scream on the cover of the magazine
Boldly declaring, "THIS IS YOUR DREAM"
Grant me Lord
Good friends
A faithful wife
A heaping share of struggle and strife
For if I am immersed in pleasure
I may forsake the greatest treasure
That lesson that I must learn
To turn
A fool full of folly
Into a child of God
If you don't believe me my friend
You'll find out bitterly in the end
When your last breath draws near
And your heart is crushed in fear
Then you will learn
What in life is truly dear
Nothing is really what it seems
Dreams

When Marianne Ran Away

It was the first time that I saw mother cry
Early morning mother entered my room
"Marianne ran away" she revealed
"Do you want to stay home from school?"
Confused, I could not grasp the concept
I was only a small child
"No" I meekly squeaked out
Mother went on "Does it hurt you?"
"It hurts mother very much"
And momma wept at the side of my bed
Sister was gone for a long while
Months on end she was away
What she did to survive I care not to think on
Eventually to simply stroll back home
In the inspection of reflection
Mare's disappearance was a barometer to measure
The great degree of displeasure
In our unhappy house
Marianne's vanishing act
Was never open for discussion
I never talked to her much about it
Perhaps a few casual statements over the years
I can only think how selfish she was
And how justified she was
She once said she wanted to take me with her
I believe she was lying
A soft sentence to fill an uncomfortable moment
In a sense I was abandoned
To the psychotic instability of my broken domain
To languish in the torment
And boil in the pain
The seeds were sown
And they have grown
Into crops insane
I have seen so much of that fruit
In every institute
I have been imprisoned in
For children are vulnerable

John Kaniecki
    And they have no say
    That's why it was so terrible
    When Marianne ran away

Sleepless Night

Music videos and wandering thoughts
I am caught
Past, present, future
Trying to understand God's hand
Prompts poems
My muse is manic like me
Forever rattling the cage in rage
But never free
Until surrender in the realization
I am a baby in a crib
Time
It is only of this domain
As is pain
On the other side
Beyond the great beyond
Where God decides to hide
All is wonderful and full of bliss
But until that sweet faithful kiss
It is more of this
Something just ain't right
Another sleepless night
Despite the tranquilizers pulsating through my veins
I contemplate my path in life
As verse depicts illogical connections
Considering the greater whole
Wondering, marveling, that I survived
And even thrived
Still lusting, coveting, crusading for more
Ever wanting the bigger score
What for?
To reach the pinnacle
And then to simply walk away
I'll get rest when the world is right
Until then
Let me say it again brother
It's another
Sleepless night

John Kaniecki

In The Greater Epic

I am
For a moment
Immortality is but a vain treasure
Sought by miserable megalomaniacs
And propagandizing pathologically lying politicians
For accepting death
Is the ultimate accomplishment of life
Not as father
Who boasted as he considered man's abstract demise
"I will discover the answer to life's greatest mystery"
But when he was hooked up on the intravenous fluids
The drippings scarcely maintaining life
The stomach cancer prohibiting eating and defecation
A skeletal, pale, face affixed in terror
"I never saw a man more scared in my life"
    Testified my wife Sylvia of our sour scarecrow
The brave, bold agnostic
Who only entered Church for funerals and weddings
Who scoffed at the Bible as contradicting fables
Calls for the Catholic Priest
It was a Saturday on Christmas Eve
The priest came, God bless his heart
It is after all his busiest time of year
There he led father in his mumbo jumbo prayers
Known as last rites
Marianne repeating the rote ritual in unison
Walter noticeably and selfishly absent
Three days later father would join mother in the grave
I cast no judgment
I dare not boast of a forecast of my day of departure
So let me talk in the terms of the ideal
To pass unto glory
Is to gather one's cherished and beloved at their side
To kiss them in kindness
To shed a tear or two for the time of separation
A weeping of joy mingling with sorrow
For there is the belief in the eternal tomorrow
Then a gust of wind blowing a candle's flame out

Polishing the Fragments

At the end to discover what life is truly about
Love and only Love
For all our roles are temporary
In the greater epic

John Kaniecki

Almost The Word Of God

There is something in poetic rhyme
Perfectly precise in time
Doctor Seuss was a visionary genius
Langston Hughes paid his dues
T.S. Eliot was the best, and dreariest
Ah if only I had some direction
I was an angry young man
Lacking Love
The American flag was truly my God above
And Jesus was only a name
Bitterness as a spice of satanic shame
Allen Ginsburg is on my headphones reciting "Howl"
I have not made the journey the journey has made me
I have transformed from an arrogant nothing
To a humble something
Grace
I went off to engineering school
"Become a lawyer, doctor or engineer"
Was father's word of advice
"Better to be an officer than an enlisted man"
His only two statements of wisdom that he shared
I am sincerely grateful he cared
There was a time when I was before the judge
Committed in a psychiatric hospital
I had a lawyer, paid for by father
"John writes excellent poetry" father declared
A sentiment he never before had shared
Later during my trial
He would speak something of great detriment
Details of the words escape me
I just recall the unbelief of my lawyer's angry glare
Wasn't he aware?
Later as I confront father for his slip of tongue
He recites an excuse
"I just wanted the judge to have all the facts"
Thaddeus you were truly an honest man
To say anything else would be to mock your greatest attribute

Polishing the Fragments

It was what made you a stellar scientist
Still you lived within a lie
For facts do not make Truth
Almost The Word Of God
An agonized cry
Drowned out by the tender sobs of a soft lullaby

John Kaniecki

Mother In The Nursing Home

Mother was a rock of support
Always advocating for my welfare
A fierce defender
Defeating the number one contender:
Apathy
She saved all of my writings in the attic
Considering them precious and priceless
Who knows one day?
Still it is the nature of humanity
To soften in the latter years
To fall into the hands of frightful fears
And so Mother was in the nursing home
After the breast cancer, the pacemaker and the stroke
We sadly learned the cancer had returned
A terminal diagnosis
Six days a week I visited her
Only absent Wednesday as Sylvia and I went to Bible study
An hour after work it was my steadfast duty
I'd sit at her side making my presence known
Lord have mercy on those abandoned alone
We'd watch the nightly news and I'd depart
Saturday Sylvia and I were all day by Mother
My wife, the marvelous cook she is, would make
Piping hot chicken soup from fresh whole chickens
Enough to last the week through
Delicious and nutritious
And Sundays it was between services
To stay a couple of hours
I did all in my power that I could do
I remember the last days
They sent mother home to die
Marianne was by her side
I got the call at four a.m. in the morning
My heart descended below the depths of Sheol
The rock had been grinded to dust
Mother had died
I cried
There is a solace

Polishing the Fragments

I was there when she needed me
A true champion she lived six months more
Than the doctors predicted
She was in the fight of her life, for her life
I did not repay what she gave me
Love keeps no score

Nature Or Nurture

Nature or nurture
This ongoing scientific debate
Is a pertinent issue upon which I relate
DNA codes overloaded astray
Or the dreaded ordeal of dismal day after day
Paranoia penetrating perverting perception
In my mind I find the immaculate misconception
Life's wicked lesson
Manic depression
Chemical imbalance
But by grand design or random circumstance?
Will my children be subjected to the curse?
Or perhaps something savagely woefully worse
Thus I speak
Am I a victim or freak?
Ah the imperfections of God's perfect plan
Scum of the Earth not worthy of the title of man
If only you would take time to descend
Or perhaps ascend
Into my unique domain
Saturated with the crimson blood of a spirit wounded in pain
Learn my concern
Turn
I defy and detest all that you hold sacred
I see your soul bare and naked
You covet gold, money, jewels
To me your end is the cruelest of cruel
And I am the Prince of Fools
For caring, sharing
Comparing all humanity
In the terms of equality
For I say this with all due respect
When your wicked deeds I inspect
I wonder what went wrong
That the entire Earth you torture
With your evil song
Nature or nurture

ON THE ROAD

From here to there
To some
Masses lost on the road to nowhere
We all have something to overcome
Wayward wanderers apathetic don't even care
Never to dirty the knee to say a simple prayer
Spinning in circles perhaps to take a tangent
Others far, far away, off of this planet
And a billion bouncing bumps of confusion
To fuel the fetters of delusion
I have an axiom
A simple truth
It matters not how far
But rather who you are
For none of mankind's roads possess equality
Born into tragic fatality
On the barren African plains fostering starvation
Or amongst fleeing refugees without a nation
Grace has its place
In directing the human race
Barefoot walking a rocky path on winter's ice
Others tanning in some tropical paradise
I examine
My feast and famine
Contradictory paradoxes
How at the epiphany of insanity
I am most free
While in the dark tormented agony of depression
I find life's sincerest lesson
So what is the conclusion?
The road goes on
When the end we reach
We shall learn what the journey needs to teach
Things one cannot utter
In simple speech

Youth

Amidst the landmines of abuse and pain
Lie pleasant pockets of pure heaven
I was after all new to this adventure called life
And there was a wide wild world to discover
It was another age with subtle secrets sealed
Waiting, just waiting to be revealed
Such is a child's duty
There was Nature in her grand beauty
Behind the row of houses
Was a wonderland of green that exists no more
Simply to turn over a stone in the soft mud
To reveal the centipedes, melee bugs
And if extremely fortunate, a sleek salamander
Mathew my childhood companion
Was adept in these woods
Knowing how to navigate his way
Through thick trees and brush
Capable of crossing the stream
Cautiously stepping from stone to stone
Avoiding the tragedy of a soaked sneaker
He would lead and I would follow
His bold spirit of adventure compelling my timid soul
    onward
Of course it was impossible to avoid
The prickly seeds that stuck on our clothes
Later we would pluck them from our person one by one
Now our entire domain is gone
Mathew and I no longer reside in the area
He has gone south hopefully to greater grandeur
To some place wholesome and pure
The trees have been cut down, massacred
To be replaced by all things, greenhouses
Whenever I drive by
Joy touches my mind
But sorrow too I find
Compelling me to weep and cry
For those who are coming before
Can learn those lessons no more

My Mirror

She is staring from the dark depths of the abyss
An oath, for better or worse, then the sealing kiss
But I never imagined this
In the throes of my manic depression
Overwhelming agonized emotion, life's worst
Swallowing the ocean, futile in quenching thirst
Never perceiving a lesson
Allowing me to say, I am strong
Not a roaring lion in rage
But a soaring eagle, a practical sage
Now Sylvia is singing a similar song
Different lyrics but an identical melody
Fortunately I know this score in every key
It has played over and over inside of my head
Until I longed that I was dead
But life with gentleness came to call
I found a flair of hope and gave it my all
To eventually achieve and thus I believe
That I can give and Sylvia receive
I envy not her iron cross
To count life a dismal loss
But I pray for moments, a flicker of joy
For the bond of Love none can destroy
My beloved wife's dementia, there is so much to learn
The road is treacherous with many a turn
Super sensitivity I dare not talk loud
Half in the past her murky mind under a cloud
Seeking a home, a world that is no longer there
Sometimes immune to all save the power of prayer
Then she would wander
Fleeing home in urgency
I ponder the sorrow of this tragedy
Longing for her home of Grenada far beyond the sea
We drive for hours keeping her calm
A soothing exercise a miraculous balm
And the worst is yet to come
So I hope and write a poem

In The Context

I am a human being
My senses not limited
By hearing, smelling, tasting, touching, seeing
For I have been planted
Into the arms of the Almighty
And He shall fight for me
You will see!
       You will see!!
              You will see!!!
How a blind man can change history
In the context of my personal past
In the context of my insanity
In the context of my sin
In the context of my struggles
In the context of these troubled times
Judge me not
For I am a shattered vase
Never knowing better days
Ever grateful for my fractured mind
My foresight is built upon Spiritual truth
My hope on the promises of my youth
I have failed
Refusal to surrender
Never to give in
It is not a game to lose or win
Rather it is a fight for the oppressed
For those God seems not to have blessed
Some of atheistic persuasion
Seize the moment of this precarious occasion
"Where is God?" they mock and hiss
"Where is God in the midst of this?"
We share our tears
We share our fears
And as the end of humanity nears
So the answer appears
But what will be the answer to the answer man?
In the context of God's plan
I will sing and shout

But tell you honestly, openly
That I too had my doubt

So Much, So Little

Facts
Data of infinite zeroes and ones
Postulations, theorems, axioms
The computer puffs fumes of gray smoke
THINKING! THINKING!! THINKING!!!
Mystical metal music makes merry melody
I reach for my hot buttered popcorn
My reality is the hottest show on cable T.V.
Metaphor
Fascism is like a row of shiny combat boots
Suckered you with a simile
I have a hole in my tooth
The government denies my dentist's request for a crown
I'd like to smile, so I do
The name of Aldous Huxley crosses the paper
The Silver Surfer serves Galactus
But Adam Warlock can steal your soul
And so Satan seduces coveting control
When every word is a lie you always have an alibi
Truth
Cool breeze on a warm night
Stars singing harmony salvation is our sweetest delight
Spirit
I throw a bottle into the eternal sea of infinity
A message of love to you from me
A trillion trillion galaxies and more
But I am more than secure
The note that I wrote
Will arrive at the exact right time
Just as sure as these words rhyme

I Hear Your Voice

A hundred honking horns
Echoing cascading in angry frustration on congested
 Broom Street
I haven't moved in half an hour
My only solace is the ever present radio
I love you; I hope you know it is so
It gives me cause to praise and rejoice
I hear your voice
When Vincent Van Gogh smoked his opium pipe
Mohammad Ali took a swipe
At each and every foe
The poetry is flowing out now
I have never written like this before
I am skirting around like a moth circling a flame
I have learned that the fire burned
But I let out a mocking laugh
Aimed at the cynical side of my better half
I am unconcerned for this is my choice
I hear your voice
Since Sylvia assumed sickness I seldom sleep soundly
Always listening for the clicking of the lock
Click!
Summoned from the land of dreams
A soldier snapping to rigid attention
As the Commander in Chief passes by
Ah the agony as she slips out the door
Into the sad domain of *nevermore?*
Her dementia so severe
There is panic, there is fear
Sylvia unable to answer her cell phone
Isolated in a busy world all alone
A good portion of the merchants on Grove Street
As well as the police cruising on the beat
Are aware
And show her special tender care
Count your blessings
But a good day is when I can say "goodnight"
To my beloved

John Kaniecki
    And say with sweet satisfaction to her reply
    "I hear your voice"

Depraved Hatred Of Dutch Demons

I remember standing waiting for the yellow school bus
I was a fragile child
Quite certain I was in kindergarten
I was in such close proximity to the house
Mother must not have thought of any danger lurking near
Waiting with the other children
The wicked monsters who belonged to their
Calvinistic religion of depraved hatred
Where God had strict rules of indoctrination
Joy seemed to be declared a grievous sin
And love was a barren desert dwelling dead within
Linda would tease and torment me
As her younger siblings would look on and learn
"Sticks and stones may break my bones"
"But names will never hurt me"
Tall Linda easily three times my size
Unable to bear this cruel taunting
I exploded with my blue plastic Peanuts lunch box
Swinging it wildly at this girl whom I detested
As she laughed in satanic glee at offending me
Donald, Linda's brother later would come to our house
Declaring boldly that a certain apple tree
Lay upon their property and not ours
This tree in question produced an ample supply of green fruit
All unfit to eat, even for a pig
But quite satisfactory to use as projectiles to hurl at one another
Depraved hatred of Dutch demons
Merciless Indian killers and slave traders
Where was your Jesus in genocide and chattel slavery?
If you are not nice
Your faith is in vain

John Kaniecki

Petition To Ban Nuclear Weapons

"Who would want nuclear weapons?" asks the man in
    all sincerity
I am taken aback at the brilliance of the concept
There was the man who carved himself in my mind
With his cold logical slashing response
An image that I will never relinquish
"See this hat?" asks the man authoritatively "Do you know
    what it means?"
I stare at foreign insignias as if the hat displays cryptic
    Babylonian symbols
"No" is my honest reply
"I would fly B-52's armed with nuclear bombs"
The policy of the United States was to always have
B-52's in the air armed with nuclear bombs
Just in case of a sneak attack?
As if our legions of missiles, submarines and secret
    satellites
Couldn't stand up to the challenge of Mutually Assured
    Destruction
Needless to say that former pilot refused to sign
But after lengthy dialogue I did get him to admit
That there are far too many nuclear weapons, an unneeded
    expense
Love of war and love of mammon seem to visit the same
    whore
I recall my frightful indoctrinated past
Where I advocated a nuclear first strike against the Soviet
    Union
That and killing Vietnamese babies if need be
After all it was better dead than Red wasn't it?
Not that I knew any details about what red was
Except that it was a color woven in the American fabric
But I was ignorant of Woody Guthrie and Joe Hill and
    life itself
The highlight of the day or more accurately the darkest
    point
Was when I approached two teenage girls

Polishing the Fragments

"Would you like to sign a petition to ban nuclear weapons, *please*?"

Please of course is the sugar on top

Baffled, the pair quizzically looked at one another

"You know big explosions, radiation lingers leaving contamination"

Nothing but a double shot of blank stares

"Hiroshima? Nagasaki?" I handed them the clipboard

It was a psychological persuasion almost borderline manipulation

The woman jotted down her name

"Why do you want my address?" she asked

"Never mind about the address" I declared mercifully

I saw no point of her getting her name on some F.B.I. watch list

I looked into the crowd for the next target

Thirty signatures I attained after an hour's effort

Sylvia was cold, anxious and wet and she as my wife was a priority

So I abandoned my work of saving planet Earth for practical efforts

John Kaniecki

Into The Future

I am sitting here creating this poem
Not trying to contemplate on what I'm writing
Sylvia needs my constant supervision and tender care
I dare not let her wander on her own anymore
God bless the merchants on Grove Street
Who would take her in as she rambled by, lost
Give her coffee, let her sit, call me on the phone to pick her up
Now she cannot find the bathroom in our apartment
I refuse to allow her to walk out on her own anymore
I haven't worked a paying job in over two years
I volunteer of course at the church
I take care of Sylvia that is more than a full time task
And I write, write, write, any free moment I can grab
Three jobs, endless hours, and not a single dollar coming in
I did sell a horror story today for all of ten bucks
It thrilled me fueling my fanciful mind with hollers of hope
They say that God tests our faith, I believe that is true
That tenet was part of the sermon that I preached today
Will the Almighty reduce me to my last dollar?
Until He smiles and hands me a wad of cash in a bestseller
Perhaps Sylvia will be sent to return home to Grenada
And I shall find employment or wind up fending for myself on the street
I ponder over life with no place to call home, in the cold, the rain, the snow
The fear of something is always worse than the reality
"I want to succeed," I shared my heart with Sylvia today
It would help to calm the agitation over my "wasted" years
While my peers were making careers and starting families
I would sit locked away, isolated in my miserable depression
Smoking cigarettes in the backyard by the massive rosebushes
Observing bees buzzing by, cursing God in my angry despair
Then I would write pouring out the words of my shattered life
Lyrics of many sorts, prolific, churning them out several

Polishing the Fragments

a day
All of them surviving the attic and then a flood in the basement
Each one copyrighted on the advice of Rose's son Billy
After all you really don't know what will be a hit do you?
I was going to thank him for his advice when I won my first Grammy
Now he and his mother have gone through the passage of death
The greatest fear is not having the ability to get my psychiatric medicine
I look at our society, cold and cruel, an inhuman juggernaut
In my broken existence I strive to shed a twinkling of wisdom
Insanity is not for individuals alone but for societies today
We possess more empty buildings than homeless people
I pray once more I can look into the future
With hope of a better world for all

Super Intelligent Fools

Once I was lost in the daze of what I proclaim was an amazing mind
While in the sixth grade I took the S.A.T. test and tried my best
My rank was consistently in the top ninety-ninth percentile
A super genius unable to make friends or to socialize
Ever present upon my face was a numb shit-eating smile
Now in inspection of reflection I realize I was far from wise
Where with all our genius are we taking this planet Earth?
Where we are born free but then become enslaved from birth
Creating, hating, debating, it's a frustrating turmoil
Destroying pristine nature bliss to plunder and spoil
European men have developed a fanatical technological machine
Science, rule of the logical mind, it is what lurks behind
This Frankenstein monster hideous and viciously obscene
We have electron microscopes and super telescopes but we are blind
Possessing intricate complexities defining sophisticated rules
We are the superior intellects correctly called super intelligent fools
On bended knee we worship the icon we claim to be the Great I Am
Lawyers twisting words like crowns of thorns create a terrible scam
Look out for number one, and to everybody else we don't give a damn
The Earth is being destroyed as digits on a computer ascend
I've got the finest of suits but what will that matter in a cataclysmic end?
I believed and received every lie that was taught in my indoctrination
I loved the United States one notch above Jesus; it was my beloved nation

Polishing the Fragments

I would have laid down my life without the slightest hesitation
Never knowing that God was showing there was so much more to his Creation
Off to Steven's Tech in dull despair without a care for the future
I wasn't doing well coping in living hell where day after day was torture
I applied myself to my studies and excelled in the academic arena
There the madness sunk in and sulking with sin my intelligence was torn apart
My brain was defiled but there was a subtle pricking deep within my heart
I inspected reality and rejected the tenets meant to enslave and control
The chemicals overflowed but it showed that I did indeed possess a soul
As does every man
For self is primary concern
Now that is an excellent lesson to learn
For we can spend trillions of dollars to wage endless war
But the true treasures beyond measure are the riches found in grace of the poor
It defies the philosophical lies that cry in the blatant prominence promoting greed
But in the end righteousness shall succeed
For all of man's inventions what can we mention that hints of redemption?
We have nuked the forest to scorn the enemy
Our utter stupidity is the final lesson

Stigma

Something just ain't quite right
It is perceptible at sight
His clothes seem to be from a distant age
As if they were the donations from an estate of some dead uncle
Far from a perfect fit they are sloppily adorned
And look at the hollow, emotionless face of stone
So they whisper and point imagining that their actions are unseen
But the dagger is stabbing repeatedly in hurt
Mentally ill is the conclusion, a.k.a. dirt
Stigma is a cross
Crucified, hung by three nails, ignorance, intolerance, and fear
Is it so terrible that this world has broken me?
Better to face the demons of reality now
Once I sought carnal perfection
Money, sex, luxury, position, style, a fine name on a tongue
I was something *special* in the days when I was young
High speed on the highway slamming into a stone mountain
I drank from the depthless waters of insanity's fountain
And the worst part
Is that in the inner recesses of my heart
All these atrocities they slander against me
I have to agree
I am my most notorious enemy
Struggling to set myself free
Fading in and out of reality
I am a fatality
Broken
In the explosion the hellfire rages
Pain casting a cryptic stain
Reborn
To reform
Refusing to be silenced I speak
I am something totally unique
Walking the opposite way of the crowd

Polishing the Fragments

Proclaiming Love's message proud and loud
If you can't be my friend because I'm mentally ill
Then fuck you Allie, you ain't worthy of my love
Cause look in the mirror and see clearer
I have concluded
That the masses are the ones deluded
And I...

Coming Of The Storm

Everybody who's not in denial sees the blackening of the sky
The winds are howling while prowling demons are scowling
An onslaught of endless pain propagated by leaders intensely vain
I witness stockpiles of nuclear weapons designed to exterminate
You really got some nerve to label me insane
I may be confused but still I know Love is better than hate
It's only a matter of time until they unleash the coming storm
I will never give in, I won't sin, I refuse to conform
There are just too many things congregating upon my plate
Some have piles of veal, a sumptuous self-indulging meal
Others are tossed a stalk of celery and are simply told to wait
Starving desperate people will risk it all, demagogues dig the deal
False hope is the deadliest drug practicality outranking the ideal
Hooray for my side, swelling with pride the rising of the tide
Do not define by political persuasion, or nationality, for you see
The primary principle of people is their pure humanity
On that appellation alone, let it be known
YOU ARE WORTHY OF LOVE!
Those who throw the dice scorn sound device, rhetoric rages
They would destroy the Earth to prove their worth
Just a chance to be a glance upon the history pages
Already the rains have brought torrential destruction to lands afar
Yemen, Syria, Iraq, Afghanistan, the victims know who they are
While twenty-two American veterans commit suicide each day

Polishing the Fragments

Peace is the path, military wrath results in a bloodbath
Poems offer little protection though they mention indisputable truth
I too once shined in the dark glory of the futile folly of my youth
I had all the answers though I really never understood any of the questions
But then reality testified and cried of lies and fabrications too absurd to mention
Patriotism is the blind dedication to this ambiguous concept called a nation
Righteousness that is the sole correct course
I feel for the refugee and for the baby born in a world torn with violence
It is only a matter of time before the crime creeps into our everyday events
Acts of terror, committed by frustrated people seeking revenge
For what it's worth here is my plea for change
Will my voice be heard above the din of madness?
Will obscurity devour and swallow blotting out making my effort amiss?
Awake oh masses, for as time passes it is harder to turn the boat
Until the message as flashing lightning declares "It is all she wrote"
Soldier lie down your weapons, it is the only cure, the only noble fight tis a war on war
Weep not child, for now is the moment to be strong
To right the wrong to sing the song
Come lend your voice to this chorus of joy before the storm comes to destroy

John Kaniecki

The Least Of These

"Whatever ye have done to the least of these ye have done unto me"
See the proud man beseeching upon his knee
Before the Lord, the Lamb of God
The God whom he deplored
The businessman looks into the eyes of those he ignored
The half starving homeless vagrants he passed on the way to the office
Where he lived a life of opulence and bliss
The rich man who lived life without a care
Never even approaching God in prayer
He mocked religion as a foolish myth
As evidence cable TV preachers obviously full of it
Besides Loving your fellow man
Would then necessitate conceiving some plan
Certainly to love the masses and then to do nil
Would be a clear violation of God's will
So life digresses into living it up with whores and cocaine
And passing idle time pretending it all isn't in vain
Vehemently protesting any notion of morality
Looking upon suckers who care with a loathing of fatality
All the while like a mouse nibbling on the wedge of cheese
The abstract notion entailing "The least of these"
So you make your martini doubly dry
And every feeling from the heart you crucify
Behind the dark tinted glass of your limousine
Others perceive that you are living the high life of the dream
Then why is every thought in your mind vulgar and obscene?
You have learned to be comfortably numb
You have won every test but you have never overcome
And so the mogul approaches the Lord on Judgment Day
He tries to speak without a single word he can say
Never come before the Lord of Lords with an empty hand
Bring him jewels of compassion that is what he does demand
For if the God of the universe is the one you seek to please

Polishing the Fragments

May I suggest passing the test
That you do your very, very best
To give comfort and aid to "The Least of These"

Indie Book Fair

Poem twenty-two for the day or there about
I was at the local Montclair library
Sitting next to Hank with his books
Of science fiction satire inspired by Douglas Adams
I had my sign up "free personal poems"
Write a poem and perhaps I'll get a sale was the strategy
A lot of smiles and thanks
But only three books sold
Sylvia had me up at four in the morning
As she announced she was leaving the house
As she digresses she is calmer, docile, as if a wounded fawn
Perhaps I've improved, I am stronger to lean upon?
A lot of my bitterness has dissipated
Still I got little sleep and I wasn't sharp
But perhaps a little fuzziness
Is something that would bless
The conception of my poetic verse
Certainly it didn't make anything worse
As bang, bang, bang, I shot them lines out
The night before I had an ample serving of doubt
Could I perform? Rise to the challenge and meet the foe
In somber reflection I would have to say so
I am searching for a kinetic reaction
To get the water boiling and then let the fires burn
Paying my dues, singing the blues, hoping on good news
Just like the thirty-five other local authors crowded in
The wheel is in spin no telling who is going to win
But to me this is no hobby or fluttering pastime
For failure you see would be a most despicable crime
Sylvia would be sent to some dismal nursing home
Sitting in her urine miserable and all alone
Or perhaps we'd separate and she'd live with her daughter
On the island of Grenada over many miles of water
My options are like a sunrise totally shrouded by storm
    clouds
I know the glory is shining but only darkness appears
As I sit exhausted typing the most dreadful of my fears
Faith in God it is a mighty and powerful tool

Polishing the Fragments

But if I am idle then I am the grandest fool
So its clickety clack, clickety clack on the keyboard
The Love of the art is truly its own reward
But the rent dear reader will be more than I can afford
All in all I must say I had a most pleasant day

John Kaniecki

On The Mountain Top With A Dirty Sky

Epiphany
A mangled metaphor maliciously making mockeries of the mad
Close your eyes to see, surrender to be free
The Whore of Babylon just declared war
I once sat upon the mountain of eternity
I would gaze into the endless infinity
The stars were my friends each with a personal name
I would kiss you with delight for each light; it was a lover's game
Then came the industrial revolution with the final solution
Money the master of mammon became the hot desire
Burning in the factories of glutton an inferno of a fire
And the byproduct of toxic fumes consumes the precious air
Mother Earth was sacred the culmination of perpetual prayer
Now the climb to Mount Zion is a capital crime
Barbed wire fence is the initial defense to keep trespassers out
I am angry but in silent defiance I slip through a hole
Laws by man are mere words on paper I only bow to my soul
Spray painted tags of defiance proclaim youthful rebellion
My spirit brags in self-reliance my tale is truthful telling
Upon the zenith where I sat at the dawn of all creation
Where the finite point erupted in jubilant celebration
An angelic chorus serenaded before us in a glorious song
It was a moment when it seemed that nothing could be wrong
But the first dawn was soon gone and night's frigid air set in
In the garden full of pardon Eve didn't believe and thus came sin
But we know that tale it has been told to old and young
It is seared into our psyche and on our lips it is sung
But to focus that on the pinnacle where I sit and ponder

Polishing the Fragments

I wonder how mortal man is scurrying and hurrying down under
In desperation I seek my former salvation and turn heavenward
But the dirty sky obscures the vision of my eye
In sobbing sorrow in woeful tomorrow tears I weep and cry
The starry host on which I used to boast upon has dissipated
The sacred melody that set me free has slipped into a silence of defiance
So here I sit upon the summit of living stone
Miserable and all alone
Ah just to have things as they used to be
Epiphany

John Kaniecki

Pumpkin Head Peter

Singing a song with the strictest meter
Hail all hail Pumpkin Head Peter
Life is merry, a fantastical game
When something goes wrong he's got a boney finger to point the blame
Like when the rhythm has been shattered
Not that it ever mattered
For you see Pumpkin Head Pete
Is a master of deceit
Trying to impress the chicks with a mouthful of lies
Sexual elisions are imperative, how badly he tries
Oh the deviant desire to do it in the bed
Gotta remember Pumpkin Head Peter got a hollow head
Drugs are his escape avoiding all responsibilities of school
Looking at those who study like they were the number one fool
For Pumpkin Head Peter though he mooches like a bum
He's got money in his family, enough to overcome
So from engineering school to rehab was his course
But Pumpkin Head Peter never had a moment of remorse
Looking back at the wild days when we used to share our room
Smoking marijuana and ingesting the magical mushroom
"We should have had some supervision"
As if learning responsibility was a satanic sin
Well anyway life continues and we journey down the path
Pumpkin Head Peter of all things teaches high school math
Also he is a lacrosse coach and a successful one at that
So to Pumpkin Head Peter I cordially tip my hat
If you just knew the character of this creep
Oh mothers and fathers of daughters and sons you would never sleep
But I am now singing the sweetest song of redemption
Something sacred that sincerely needs a mention
For in the course of the journey the potter molds the clay
We can never be defined solely by our dark yesterday
Pumpkin Head Peter repented he truly changed his course

Polishing the Fragments

But I wonder what remains in the brains that is the source
Always finding the fault in the external
Infernal!!
For if Pumpkin Head Peter had been born black in the hood
I am certain in life that he wouldn't have fared so good
Pumpkin Head Peter has dissipated to a Facebook page
He gets angry when I present to him the reality of this age
The cycle of endless war and the unprecedented danger never seen before
But it ain't Pumpkin Head Peter's fault that we all know for sure
Smiley face!! (of a pumpkin head)

John Kaniecki

First Time In A Committed Psychiatric Ward

It's not sane to think that you are going crazy
In reflection looking back there were signs more obvious than the noonday sun
Going to the United Nations on Manhattan Isle with a smile
And declaring I had a message from God would certainly be one
Saint Clare's was a small restricted unit under lock
Perhaps with only a dozen patients at maximum capacity
So confined that if I weren't paranoid I would have become claustrophobic
I was given a hefty dose of Thorazine several times a day
The horse tranquilizer propelled with my immense anxiety
The drug would cause my tongue to rigidly extend causing excruciating pain
I was a spectacle of the whole crew of staff and patients
It was an "us" versus "them" atmosphere
Never being released was an ominous and constant fear
The excessive boredom drove me into smoking cigarettes
I the all-time loser finally had to pay up on all of his bad bets
Group therapy was an effort in hostile humiliation
The psyche techs would prod us to reveal our intimate flaws
As they navigated the ship of conversation as some pure Madonna
If ever I possessed a single-minded captivating desire
If I say I sought anything but release I would be an immense liar
There are no adequate words to express
The massive deflation of ego to despair beyond helplessness
I was the crazy tramp that proper society despised
An outcast relegated to the periphery one rung below the drug addict
Perhaps I had finally bottomed out
It was a crisis of immense proportions a triple red alert

with no doubt
But Captain Kirk and the rest of the Enterprise
Were unwilling to do what only God could realize
It was the start of a perilous journey
I was crawling naked on my hands and knees on a barbed wire path full of glass
Even now after twenty-nine years have faded into the past
The events are found profound inside of my wounded mind
In insanity I shed the shades which were making me blind
I found the priority in a wholesome existence is simply being kind
To your faith add goodness
In reflection my inner poet had been emancipated
For the severe affliction had inadvertently created
An advocate, nay a champion to wage war against everything I hated
So if you see a man talking to himself in clothes shabby
Remember that perhaps it is somebody exactly like me full of sensitivity
Take caution for point of view defines reality
One day we will commit the bankers, generals, weapon makers and their ilk
To reprogram their feast of fury with a mellow mild milk

John Kaniecki

Picture Perfection

Picture perfection
The qualities you mention
The image that forms inside your mind
Will reveal if you see or if you're blind
I hope perfection was kind
Was he wearing a business suit?
Or some big breasted beauty looking real cute?
Jesus?
Was he white?
If he was that just ain't right
Was there green?
Was it money or nature serene?
Question after question
Picture perfection
Super feminine
Would a wholesome mother be a sin?
Now can you put a face to the selected grace?
I'll bet nobody selected somebody mentally ill
Still
Is there room for me in the inn?
Or must I too be forced into a stable?
Or perhaps you consider the Bible just an elaborate fable
Intelligent
Perfection could never be dumb
How about wisdom?
Carnal or spiritual?
Picture perfection
Why in this poetic presentation?
"Whatsoever ye have done to the least of them ye have
 done unto me"
Reality
Philosophy
Practicality
That we are all of worth
And we need to share this Earth
Thus I open my life for inspection
Picture perfection
My flaws, my warts, my sincere honesty

Polishing the Fragments

I desire to drive you in the proper direction
Picture perfection
Your answer will clearly explain
If you are living life in vain

John Kaniecki

Loose Wire

How many times do I check the stove and the lights?
Sometimes to drive a few blocks and then turn around
Nervous paranoia infesting my brain
As if my skull were a nest of angry wasps
Each one stinging with a bitterness of doubt
We human beings were never machines
Still my irrational desire could be classified as a loose wire
Some circuit overloading my mind exploding
Into a virtual realm where illogical rules dictate the norm
Check and double-check, I just have to be sure
And I'll do it a few times more
Sadly I have not found a cure
But rituals tend to bring a calming effect
Rote repetition bringing a freeze to my wavering ambitions
No diagnosis for a root cause
Though psychiatrists pontificate over Freudian slips
Psychology so mystical that it is barely a science
Case in point psychotropic medications
There is no rhyme or reason or complex equations
Rather the effectiveness is discovered by trial and error
I am a lab rat to be tested upon
Poked and prodded and above all scrutinized in careful observation
The psych ward is after all called a behavioral unit
Businessmen who sacrifice family to accumulate masses of mammon
Their carnal wisdom is never called into question
Do not I have a right to reject all the conventionalities of the day?
After all the world is teetering on the precipice of cataclysmic destruction
If it be global warming, nuclear war, or the general man's inhumanity to man
I am told to be silent, keep my place and to go along with the plan
Never mind everyone from history I admire was a rebel
From Jesus on down they stood up to the system in fierce opposition

Polishing the Fragments

Some laying it all on the table paying the ultimate sacrifice
If you have inclinations that authority is not seeking humanity's welfare
I have then to offer some tender advice
First of all I shall commend you for the first step, a genuine care
Never stare into the eyes of the abyss or gaze upon its shadow
For to see the evil in its entirety is truly a fatal blow
Rather see the truth that each part possesses a similar heart
For Love is a mighty weapon that can wound
But the same sword also has the ability to mend and heal
Your soul, the mettle of your determination, is tried upon the fire
Perhaps one day to fuse together my loose wire

An Interlude

A gray-haired man with his greasy frazzled strands claiming eccentricity
He looks up towards the orchestra tuning their instruments
The Stradivarius cackles alongside others of the finest quality
It sounds like a fatally wounded demon wailing doubly in pain and remorse
When the final moment comes how many abandon course?
But the instructor with fury scribbles with ink and pen
Here there appears an opportunity that won't come again
The erratic genius has composed a symphony of exquisite beauty
Unfortunately the conductor has left his copy in the pocket of his other jacket
So with selected vision he perseveres above the racket
On the couch Sylvia sits snoring away
It has been yet another trying day might I say
Which brings about the insight what am I trying to accomplish
I have rubbed the Genie's bottle and have been granted a wish
My life has been shattered into fragments
Committed at age twenty, two months is a life sentence
Stigmatized, demonized, agonized, mesmerized
Poetry
The score is far from pure
And I ever the artist miserably insecure
I am taking a chance, a little romance with the unknown
Perhaps in time historians will reflect on how I as a poet have grown
Then again, I may be fueled with nuclear powered delusion
That there is a minute possibility of success is but an egotistical illusion
Still with a manic fury I create and propagate
Surrender can only render a warrior defeated
My money supply will soon be depleted
I would have to send Sylvia to Grenada with a one way

ticket
For her to stay with her eldest daughter Marilyn
To me you see it would be the ultimate sin
But I have faith in God, a God who is gentle and kind
Despite the fact that He blew my mind
Or allowed it to happen
I am mincing words, slicing the onion with various techniques
If His eye is on the sparrow and he numbers every hair on my head
He could have taken me by another path instead
So I search for the meaning in the mental illness
How the incredible curse can transverse and bless
I will find out when the band begins to play what has been composed
As of yet I say without regret you haven't seen the best of it
Allow me to be rude and conclude this brief interlude

The Great Beyond

Babies are intensely focused
Mysteries abound in the mundane let alone exciting
But we grow and come to know our peers a world apart
I remember in the first grade I asked somebody for a piece of candy
"Would you give me some if you had some?" they asked
"No" was my honest and selfish response
I never got candy and needless to say I had very few friends
But that's not how the story ends
Love, it was as elusive to me as the word's definition
Shackled with self-doubt, crippled by inhibition
Nervous, combing my hair a different way every morning
Whispers of haters, the searing words scorning
Paranoid my mind was destroyed by intense fear
Shortest boy in my class, I could not pass without danger lurking near
But maturity came; I found confidence in the refuge of others
Marc and Steve, they became close, we were tight like brothers
And then off to engineering school with a brand new slate
I reinvented John, gone was the bitter man, something new to recreate
Joined a fraternity with all its talk about brotherly love
The message was received and believed
But a year down the line things weren't fine how I grieved
Getting drunk seven days a week, my the times were bleak
The star student's GPA plummeting now barely passing
I applied the fraternal harmony to all human beings
    I mourned for the unfortunate; anything else would make love counterfeit
And then I heard about Jesus
Soon I overcame the alcohol and nothing was ever the same
Then after hitchhiking across the United States the ultimate crash came
COMMITTED
I was at the top of my game

Polishing the Fragments

Still I have an agitated finger wondering exactly who to blame
My screaming mother and an indifferent father coldly cruel
The host of bullies and the cast of hundreds frighteningly cool and cold
Or perhaps the harsh hazing of my fraternity had a hold
But I have learned to forgive and live, it is the Way so I Am told
I have ventured into the spiritual domain
The fearful introvert unable to talk to a stranger
Has in bliss dismissed any kind of cold and indifferent danger
My cross it has been heavy but still I have found it fond
For it has launched my psyche to understand the great beyond
That the center of the universe is always I
And thus the knowledge to understand the desperate cry

Haunting Dreams

One level under an outright nightmare
The callous creepy basement above the dangerous dungeon
Pricking on some memory lingering as an ember
Churn the memories and the flames will evoke
Gray dusty mellow smoke
Making me choke
Never graduating from engineering school
Torments me as in my fantasy I return
Or perhaps some fair love who abandoned me
When I was struck with my insanity
And she never to show the slightest bit of concern
"Goddamn mental patient"
Walter's words, so much for brotherly love
All because he left his small son in front of the television unsupervised
After all he was busy playing games on the computer
And I had to rebuke his lax behavior of irresponsible danger
The visions seem so real
Perfect evidence that there is so much more for me to heal
Many lessons, many rivers, caught in the maze, a myriad of hells
Who knows what tomorrow tells?
Perhaps some other aspect to cast eerie spells
Perverted, unconverted, dispirited
Of all of God's creations most magnificent is the human mind
From its fountains flow fabulous fancies forever to find
Imagination, salvation, inspiration, temptation
Forcing to function despite satanic seduction
Voiceless screams experiencing haunting dreams
Life is never what it seems
For all I have overcome what have I become?
A shell of a man who can never compare to the standard set out there
Never to be normal
A victim of an acute leprosy rotting at the core of my brain

Polishing the Fragments

Infernal, insane, and here I sit in an exercise intensely vain
And when I direct my vision at the shadows scant light does remain
This is but a shard of the vase
With gentle fingers I pick up the piece
Painted upon it is a smiley face flourishing in grace
In a moment I kiss the universe and feel a quasar's caress
Release
Some people would trade all they possess for a moment of peace

A Poet's Pain

When I received my high school directory I listed myself as a poet
At the time I considered my selection better than unemployed or mentally ill
I always hurt; it just took a long time to realize my inner agony was abnormal
That the abuse, teasing, mockery, bullying wasn't universal
Now I seek to liberate the world from every single force of oppression
I have learned reality and have digested the brutal lesson
So I write poetry hoping to inspire
That somehow in a spiritual way to ignite a wholesome fire
That among the world there should be an ambiguous equality
That the culture of "third world" nations is perhaps more valid than our own
From selfish rebels to world exploiters so this nation has grown
I take no pride in Native American genocide
Go to the source any force of evil must be denied
And in the process rip to shreds the smug arrogant pride
That self-aggrandizing declaration that this nation's military can intervene
Wherever, whenever and against any enemy its foggy eyes have seen
It is not okay to spend trillions to kill in aggressive war
While billions suffer from hunger and people are poverty stricken poor
I have meandered off the straight and narrow far from my rhymes
I focus on meaning, obvious as a June moon bellowing with sacred chimes
That there is righteousness and war is one of man's foulest crimes
Yet in easy contentment society is placated into a deceitful lull
It's not my kids going to die; besides such things are out of my control

Polishing the Fragments

I believe in the masses, I believe in the power of Love, I believe in the example
I have fought the system claw and fang though I am presently obscure
When motivated millions make many moves the impact is sure
I throw my withered scarecrow frame across the gears of the machine
For the demagogues are blaspheming in heated rhetoric of hatred most obscene
With blood and oil they grease the slashing juggernaut
Killing you dirty or killing you clean do you know what I mean?
And in the midst of the red, red rain
A cry asking why so many innocents must perish and die
I observe the cruelty in society how lives are flawed, empty and vain
From deep within wickeder than the worst sin is a poet's pain
For I have no power to make a change but rather to simply explain
So I write and fight in words that shimmer and glimmer in delight
For with hope I think about the slim chance that I just might
Inspire an entire generation to be conscious of the world's ways
That the government is not our master and only our ideals should we praise
All in all leading the call so that we may arrive collectively at better days
While that dark choice seeks to silence my voice quoting "you are insane"
A poet's pain

The Great Critic

I remember how as a child we would go to the park for a picnic
Some fried chicken, watermelon, and of course the lemonade
"I cannot read your work, without sounding rude or insensitive"
And thus pontificates the self-proclaimed great critic
Pissing in the wind, and living to simply let live
You see Lilliputians abound, everywhere they are found
The ants are marching single file in a straight and narrow line
Sharing, caring none of them calling their plunder mine
This is not an attack I am simply turning the other cheek
But it gives me a moment that I can calmly speak
I have heard endless critics declare their message divine
Always it was some criticizing of the life that was mine
I was too this or too that, and of course they had the solution
The ultimate rape of the mind was being in an institution
Twenty-four hour intense observation to kill what I held dear
That it was abnormal that I didn't want to be an engineer
Ah how the doctor installed in me a dreaded dark fear
I was to conform to the norm; that was made viciously clear
After years of deep honest contemplation I have seen the light
I have discovered that love and kindness are always right
I remember Jesus giving his Sermon On The Mount
With so many in attendance the number none could count
There he broke five barley loaves and two small fish
Feeding all, he did what was impossible to accomplish
And for his immeasurable kindness and infinite love they nailed him to a cross
THEY NAILED HIM TO A CROSS BETWEEN TWO THIEVES
I am a fool, one of them who sincerely believes
I take the message in its totality

Polishing the Fragments

And yes indeed I love my enemy
Satan is always coming trying to water down the wine
Pick and choose what you want to use that is just mighty fine
The harsher the critic the more the hater
Art is beautiful a merry trip and in truth there is nothing greater
Living life well that is the ultimate expression
You see in every moment in some fashion there is a lesson
I guess bullies with their putrid mess of words will continue
To change the entire world there is so little that I can do
I will take those offensive comments and allow them to inspire
I will kill the cold of what was told and ignite a ferocious fire
The great critic why she thinks that she is something so grand
Understand?

Driving Dementia

Up late writing, up early trying to keep Sylvia from meandering away
Unable to use her cell phone anymore she could wander anywhere
Some of the police know her by sight and the neighborhood is safe
Still you don't take your diamonds and cast them anywhere near swine
I can only rest if I know that my sweetest Sylvia is doing just fine
The tricks the mind triggers tremors of tremendous tragedy
But when we are driving in my car calmness captivates my wife
I wonder in her silence what is happening in the recesses of her life
I know that most of the time she doesn't recognize our own home
It is what prompts the rat-gnawing agitation that makes her roam
I have driven thousands of miles in every single direction
I know more out of the way paths then I could possibly mention
Confident of the major highways I chance upon a curvy back road
As fall approaches the forests are full of colors that explode
And Sylvia is content to allow the world to whiz on by
Sometimes in somber sadness I seek solace to cry
But I must be brave and I must be strong
When your true love has dementia it is so easy to be wrong
A harsh word or a thoughtless accusation could bring wrath
Sometimes I am totally innocent but I bathe in her anger's bath
Most of the time I am sincerely guilty of the crime
Perfection is the calling that I need to give proper care
But I'd settle for gentleness and to always be aware

Polishing the Fragments

I dare not go for the long rides over the highways any more
My car's condition is tenuous at best and I feel most insecure
But every day we're on our way just like the day before
First stop is Quick Check for some delicious flavored coffee
All the staff sees me and laugh as they all know me
Then it's a bagel usually to fill our stomachs for the ride
The trek to me is exceptionally exciting if it's a road I never tried
But those choices are narrowing down almost extinct
All the while with a gentle smile upon my stories I think
Perhaps in the future God will bless and I'll have much more to offer
If millions of dollars come down the path perhaps I'll hire a chauffeur
So until the bestseller rocks the free world with sensation
I will drive the roads offering momentary salvation
It is a tiresome task but I don't ask for my cross to be tossed
Rather I ask that I have strength so I won't faint and Sylvia won't be lost
Every road has a toll but each with a different cost
Driving dementia is something hard but then easy to do
Driving dementia coming to a theatre near you
Only offered by the chosen few

Our Garden

Sylvia was famous for having the most marvelous garden
  in the universe
That is hyperbole but so many of the others were clearly
  worse
We had tomatoes, peppers, lettuce, scallions, raspberries,
  flowers galore
It was quaint, beautiful, vibrant in life, I couldn't ask for
  more
Sylvia would rise before the sun to till the precious soil
It was a labor of love, tending the garden spending her toil
Now the garden is not so neatly organized
It has been dilapidated as weeds have begun to mix in
It is a wild combination of righteousness and vile sin
In the center of the garden we buried Trixie our dog
Besides a couple of fish she was the only pet we ever
  possessed
It was my father's and when he was dying it was his desire
That Sylvia and I would take care of his precious animal
For a good number of years it was simply wonderful
But life is a cycle inevitably turning into death
There is for every creature a first and a last breath
Over Trixie's resting place sits a most unorthodox plant
It is large like unto a tree with large leaves and berries
It is a perennial every year to reappear
Beside it stands a tall plant with spikes on the edges of
  its leaves
It intrigued me so I nurtured it to see how it would grow
At the end of the season purple flowers come out
There is something good in all of us that I do not doubt
It is only a matter of time before the goodness will sprout
All that is needed is the tender care, the water and sunlight
But alas so many pass into death's domain doing nothing
  right
Selfishness is a pesticide that chokes the beauty hidden
  inside
This same wild brush has spread throughout our little plot
It flourished with tiny purple flowers crying out not to
  be forgot

Polishing the Fragments

Sylvia harvested an armful and set them on the table in a vase
Her labor of years before is rewarded with a blessing of grace
Eden they say was a place so good it defined paradise
We can never return to that place, heed my advice
Heaven is the direction where we as a people must journey
We have knowledge, and innocence is something always lost
Experience by the nature of the road has a toll with a cost
Unfortunately so many on Earth never even learn their lessons
Reason being they are always asking the wrong questions
How can I make money? How can I make the bigger score?
It would be funny but it takes humanity into endless war
Instead in humble devotion we should be seeking for pardon
Down on your knees is common when tending a garden
Sylvia has planted a seed of love deep inside my heart
It will grow forever even the moment when death makes us part

You Sing The Blues

Ruthie is a child growing up and that in itself is difficult enough
Somehow I see in my reality that now the world is really tough
George and Marlese her parents had Sylvia and I over for Thanksgiving
It's sad to be grown and on your own it isn't a good way to be living
There should be family, and all society extended kinfolk
But in the United States our existence is a cruel joke
Where trillions are spent on war and the impoverished we deplore
Which brings me to Ruth who is a youth that speaks the truth
Coming now to be aware in a time of glaring hate
If only I could scream and invoke a dream telling life to wait
Racism, sexism, war, poverty those things aren't good news
So I tell sweet little Ruthie when life has got you down
When you can't manage a smile and barely resist a frown
There is one thing that you do, you sing the blues
I say Ruthie you're going to grow up to be a musical star
We sing in the church building, "Yes Jesus Loves Me"
And silly songs that I create ad lib spontaneously
Brother Jones laughs at my little singing group of girls
But when they're famous and rich Jones will only get paltry cash
I am sure Ruthie and Anna and Nadia will one day be a smash
They already are in the eyes of the Almighty
And in the end my friend don't pretend that anything else matters
The most materialistic miser would offer all he possessed for one more hour
For death is supreme in its hand is the ultimate power
That makes the bravest of men whimper and cower
Don't be fooled by Hollywood heroes made of celluloid
Their bodies are flesh and they too will be destroyed

Polishing the Fragments

There is a disconnect between the rich and the poor
And sweet Ruthie and others like her they are the cure
Respectful children, full of life and love
Except when the dark clouds gather in the heavens above
A rain of pain is soon to fall I can hear the distant call
Empires rise, soar in the skies, tell blatant lies and then stall
But when Washington burns one learns lessons very cruel
The rich will sacrifice everyone else's sons playing the fool
But Ruthie will never go and kill for the empire
At least I hope and pray every day that won't become her desire
In a world where our nuclear missiles are called Peace Keepers
But only those in our own possession of course
In the hands of our foes they are the worst of the worst
Ruthie maybe one day you will be taking a college class
And be studying poetry of a most relevant age
When you are please refer to this work and show them this page
Life is always paying your dues so I say "You sing the blues"

Peace Action

Nuclear weapons are the definition of insanity
A weapon if used existence would become total vanity
As those not killed in the immediate blast
Would perish from the radiation that would linger
When they push the button that day it will be our last
May God prevent that wicked finger
Unfortunately I cannot handle all the world's problems just now
But it bothers me, this endless war, we must fight it somehow
So Sylvia and I volunteer at Peace Action
It keeps us busy for the morning and brings sweet satisfaction
I am not the solution; the solution is in the example
Emulate what you would recreate, take what is wonderful
The rest just dump into the big blue sea of forgetfulness
Sail on your merry own way in your righteous bliss
May the sun always shine and the waves be calm
And while we're at it pray that they never drop the Bomb
I seek the perfect world where peace and love prevail
I seek the perfect self but every day I fail
So we send out our flyers and plot out our ambitions
We go to the local fairs and have people sign petitions
It is futile for us to resist the awesome war machine
But we are a rare lot us that hold fast to the dream
We never let reality get in the way of what we believe
Despite impossibility every day we achieve
For the world is changed one mind at a time
And thus the purpose and the intent of this rhyme
Mankind was never meant to be divided
We were to share of the garden and all God has provided
Rich and poor that dear friend is a grand mistake
For some are pigs and greedily gobble down all they can take
While emaciated others gnaw on roots or cakes of dirt
Cannot you understand the magnitude of the hurt?
When you steal from the poor you are mocking God for sure

Polishing the Fragments

It is greed indeed that comes to feed the need for war
Profits are paramount never mind the body count, more,
    more, more
Ah can you not see what you are to hate and deplore
I search for the answer I seek the heavens for the cure
And then I look inside and ask "What have you done?"
As long as I try I will never die, I know victory will be won
One day I may be famous or remain forever obscure
But of this sole fact I am certain and firmly secure
That God will cleanse the heavens and Earth with fire
Frustrating the rich's diabolical desire
And then we shall be pure

Hallelujah

A good thing will bring a blessing from the King
For a song I will surrender my soul
It's all in the lyrics and in the voice exhibiting control
For words they are Truth
Truth never comes in a disguise and God, He never speaks any lies
So much for all the treaties given to the Indigenous Natives
I understand stolen land it takes command in the mind of the damned
In all simplicity
I will fight to be free
For I have forsaken all carnal hope in this Waste Land
T.S. Eliot had technical expertise but Langston Hughes I understand
Everybody is so hot for the newest trend
It's a revolving door to heaven the journey it never really does end
As sufferers in Hell hope for a mercy that never will come
When the time to cry came by they remained deaf, blind and dumb

JESUS

I'll never surrender cause I ain't a pretender
I'll serve with the best Love I can render
All my days let me sing a song of praise in a wild frenzied craze
I can abandon sense and reason cause faith prompts treason
They can't break me no more I'm already shattered
It'll be hard to pass my guard across the universe my soul has been scattered
I will fight with my cross I have already counted all for a loss
I can't be fired or retired cause I'm my own boss
Insanity has its merits like a Get Out Of Jail Free card
But Satan has a monopoly on his favorite currency called agony

Polishing the Fragments

You see possessions enslave and hound your heels to the lonely grave
There is only one name that can save
So we bring tidings from our King and succinctly sing Hallelujah
I am a sinner
And David he was the ultimate winner
He would never deflate footballs or pay umpires to make the wrong calls
But he was a cold-blooded killer
His horror was a chiller
This is the lesson shining clear as the sun on the day time began
Forgiveness necessitates that there is some dark mark
And on that somber note I end the quote and disembark

The Sin Of Poverty

There is a war of the classes and as time passes
The rift grows and nobody knows which way the wind blows
For Mister Money sailing the sunny seas upon his yacht
The plight of the poor is never known let alone forgot
In his mind you will find that he is willingly blind
With Darwinian concepts of survival of the fittest
His soul is bankrupt and his affections counterfeit
For his care is only for his treasures of mammon
While in the African outback and West Virginia there is famine
The upper one percent refuses to repent
Yet they claim that Jesus Christ was heaven sent
"Sell all that you have and give to the poor" is it unclear what he meant?
Almighty God is patient with a will we cannot comprehend
I would be a liar if I didn't proclaim His desire that each should be a friend
The rich as an insatiable whore steal all the more refusing to mend
In serpent sermons false prophets condemn the poor in Puritan Pride
But when the true God comes around them rich people had best hide
Poverty is not a sin!
The accumulation of material wealth is not the way to win
Rather to serve mankind in a bond of Love
If you disagree with me you shall see when God intercedes from above
For the hour is late and the freight train locomotive called deathly hate
Is running down the tracks rambling like a charging bull with no control
For you cannot talk mercy and grace with one who has sold their soul
I have seen them in the warehouse these temporary workers for hire
All week long wearing one shirt and that's certainly not

Polishing the Fragments

from personal desire
Meanwhile limousines pick up the clientele mostly the owner's family
This should not be
Where is the cry for justice? Why does silence permeate the land?
Do not the fools in folly have a notion to understand?
That the worker is the foundation of the very nation
And when he's cheated and treated with disdain we are a castle built on sand
They lie to make money and that is not funny
Oh if we could just afford to pay you a little more
But it is the same sad sack story they've spoken hundreds of times before
But hey they will bring the leftovers from their private feast
A token in the lunchroom, a gift to those who are the least
One day the streets will be red with blood
As the tide of the masses rise in an overwhelming flood
As Langston Hughes sings the blues and Emmett Till cannot lay still
All in all hear the call and understand that God has a will
It is not to maximize profits at all cost
Rather it is to seek and save those who are lost
The elite of the world are satanically crazy as they profess the sin of poverty

John Kaniecki

Whitey's On The Moon

They are rapping in the ghetto which is now called the hood
Them white folks all say that it's immoral and no good
But their sons go gangsta at least not while at school
And they'll wander downtown just to be treated cruel
By some Crip hanging out on the corner trying to cope
Whitey will come on down and buy himself some overpriced dope
Jamming on the C.D. to something that is outer space
Cause they still believe in the "great white race"
Never mind in the mirror it is clearer who is the disgrace
But there is an element, a moment that they strive to grasp
They are petting the little puppy but it's a rat with teeth like an asp
Well they blame every fault in their society on the poor
But they are glad to have them go and fight Wall Street's war
They wave the flag, boast and brag, but not so secretly deplore
When the warrior returns, he quickly learns, the fire burns
As coked up traders score with whores to celebrate rising numbers
Meanwhile in grandest style God in His heaven silently slumbers?
Maybe He's seeing how sadistic our overlords can really get
They crucified the Son of God that I will never forget
So when they tell me that He's coming real, real soon
I sit back and relax and remember, Whitey's On The Moon
I am stealing a line from Gil Scott of course
Cause according to Al he is the rapper's number one source
I see Whitey talking indignantly about how the system is rigged
Slavery was a long time ago, don't you dig?
As if Jim Crow was some kind of pleasurable poetic piece
As if the traps of racism fell and the hell offered some release
But the Piper was piping as Emmett Till's mother was

Polishing the Fragments

weeping to his tune
But forget the regret cause Whitey's on the Moon
Hell no, scream the poor white trash cause they can't collect decent cash
The elite with venom sweet point to the man with the darker skin
He is the fault; blame them for everything evil that is your sin
So not too bright, they fail to see the light that the rich divides
Behind various ambiguous walls, the master he hides
Politicians are but a face to the disgrace but lack the real power
You'll find out who's in Satan's mind when we come to the revealing hour
Remember in the anti-December the solstice comes in the month of June
But have no fear, there is no atmosphere, just ask, Whitey's On The Moon
Can't pay the rent, and I'm too stubborn to truly repent
So here let me end calling out to my friends, you know who you are
I ain't on the Moon; rather I am hanging in a bar on Jupitar

John Kaniecki

Satan's ABC's

Lie
Swear to God, on your mother's grave on apple pie
Everybody is a sucker to be set up for a swindle
Manipulate and get them to hate, conquer and divide
Yourself is the only one truly on your side
When all else fails, brutal, vicious violence prevails
But there is an art to the deal
Develop a system of trust, it is a must
Take them for all they're worth, steal even Mother Earth
Give them the haunting impression they have learned their lesson
The exterior is superior
It matters naught what is caught in the inner workings of self
Put your conscience, your morals, your heart and soul on the shelf
Always claim to be number one
Every war it must be won
If you doubt then there is all more the reason to scream and shout
In the end none of it makes any sense
Suppress the shame and guilt cause your thrill comes at another's expense
If caught pretend to be ignorant
Develop a clever phrase to use in the darkest of days
"It depends on what the definition of the word 'is' is"
Mockery, slander, whispering and the winking of the eye
Question everything with a distorted "why?"
When you say something demand that everyone comply
Create sophisticated theories like "Social Darwinism"
Use grand and lofty labels, such as "Manifest Destiny" to disguise sin
You can shift consistency it matters not at all
Being hypocritical is fine as long as no one calls you out
"Laissez Faire" simply means you don't care
Keep the truth "Top Secret" until a couple generations have passed by
Then casually admit what happened with a gentle sigh

Polishing the Fragments

Take all that you desire, flesh for fantasy
When pressed for a commitment say "I was born to be free"
Deny any responsibility but taking all credit is fine
When questioned about anything declare yourself divine
If pressed make up a convenient alibi
Lie

John Kaniecki

The Lesser Of Two Evils

Death by riots or death by nuclear war?
But the end is for sure
Barring some freaky fantastic fabulous anomaly
Something like the dice rolling off of the table
Perhaps Cain not killing Abel
Clearly we are sinking to a new low
Other ships beside the Titanic sunk you know
Like the General Slocum
No matter how you measure disaster in the end it is the same
Plenty of agony and a second helping of shame
So we have two candidates running for the highest office
This a snapshot for future generations
Wondering why the upcoming disaster for a host of the world's nations
We don't realize that we are inside of Nazi Germany
Cause despite all our flaws the masses believe the T.V.
Those of us wise with open eyes see through the disguise
It's a sadistic game when you look into the mirror you see the same
We will elect a beast that is a guarantee
Whether it is Donald or Hillary
A dark, dismal, diabolical day
When you borrow from the devil you eventually gotta pay
America is living on borrowed time
Righteousness dictates that none can ever escape a crime
Understand that we have so much blood on our hands that we are damned
For if we reap a tenth of what we have sowed
New red rivers would be overflowed
Vote for the lesser of two evils is the wise declaration
Go hold your nose and then vote without hesitation
Like taking a poisonous pill, don't let it linger in your mouth
Cause you just might spit it out choking on doubt
So where were you when so much hung in the balance?
Did you spin the wheel of fortune and bet it all on a chance
Today I went to the farmer's market with Peace Action

Polishing the Fragments

To get a petition signed to spend less on the military
Our democracy is a hollow shell of a miserable mockery
For the population turns a blind eye to the cry of those perishing
We debate who the better basketball player is today
We scrutinize football statistics but a "war on terror" is okay
Unending and ambiguous
And nobody truly understanding the message of Jesus
The lesser of two evils let it sink in
The lesser of two evils a most miserable sin
Neither way do we win

Words

Star spangled rhetorical infernal opulent condemnations
In the beginning was the Word
Now in a plurality of denominations they pander salvations
Thanx God for spell-check and sublime respect
Distorted misreported extorted and then they get deported
On a lie
Oh hear a mother's lonesome wail as her baby does die
Lament sent calling on the ambiguous Almighty to repent
Words written, words spoken, words weren't made to be broken
Tell that to the authority, man you're joking
But treatise with lawyer language legalize comes a begging please
Never mind the spirit you can only hear it when they come with bayonets
One day I say you'll pay all the day with multiple regrets
Now a musical interlude could be rude and crude
But when you sing a song them words come on powerful and strong
But you can only receive it if you believe it
I used to sing the blues but I heard the news and I got the grays instead
What's the grays you say?
It's just like the blues except some dismal rain is going to drop down your way
You look up to the sky and you just wanna cry
Cause not only can't you see heaven but you wish you had the blues
Hurry don't worry the banker he owns the casino and the machines are rigged
Dig?
Jazz is the triumphant trembling of a trumpet
As the British are civilized with tea and crumpet
As they conquer and kill for little more than a cheap thrill
Of course euphuisms are one way solutions a twisting of the truth
They proclaim lies blind the eyes fooling the gullible youth

Polishing the Fragments

And if the reality by some chance of circumstance
    happens to dance
Where life takes on a wife in the sweetest of romance
Nuances
Schrödinger's Principle you can never have a perfect beat
    or a perfect rhyme
Simultaneously
Poets are wordsmiths or so they claim
But writers weren't born equal in fact no two are ever
    the same
Like snowflakes
Except some are outright fakes
So you heard about the word from the wicked to the
    absurd
My fear is that I ain't clear in my obvious smear

The Perfect Ten

The perfect ten
Not a nine point eight
It is the ultimate score at the Olympics
When the audience is awed into excited "ooohs" as the gymnast competes
Even the other countries cannot help but be amazed
And applaud their sworn bloodthirsty enemy
In the world of a dementia caregiver a perfect ten
Is required day after day, hour into hour, through endless weeks
Even then it perhaps will not suffice
And so what happens when I dismount from the parallel bars
Landing incorrectly and breaking my leg!
Remember the athletes competing have had years of intense training
Rising early before the sun with grueling workouts
A myriad of coaches giving precious insights of wise trinkets
A whole host of competitions where the worst are sifted out purged away
Leaving at the end the most skilled performer
And then in a once in a lifetime event they execute a magical miracle
Meanwhile I am yelling at Sylvia for peeing on the floor
How quickly I forget that her mind is so much like a child's
I am not prepared for this
I never took a course in dementia care giving in college
But the good Lord is looking over me
Even a relatively small blessing, a day at church
Or even hours away when Sylvia visits with a friend
They are precious moments of emancipation
For I am a slave chained to the galleys always rowing
Unfortunately the boat which is on fire is rapidly sinking
Sharks are circling in the waters grinning razor-sharp teeth in starvation
I can hear the play-by-play of the biased announcers
"There is John getting awakened from the couch by a noise"

Polishing the Fragments

"Thrust into reality as Sylvia is peeing on the floor"
Quickly to the bathroom I take her far too late
Only to discover that her absorbent underwear is not on
The volcano erupts!!
If only, I yell and scream
Not for a moment but my terrible tirade lasts a good half hour
The day before Sylvia was running out of the house
I can't let her get lost in the cold
She can't even find her way from the bedroom to the bathroom
I pull her orange jacket and she falls to the ground
"You hurt my back" she complains
And my tears can't be held back any longer
I wish somehow I could be perfect if only I were stronger
But then again who can be a perfect ten every single time

The Twist

Emily Dickenson is the exception
How many geniuses existed that get absolutely no mention?
Brilliant in verse subjugated to that creative curse
It is a load of iron and steel that us poets must bear
It is a tremendous burden to feel the universe tremble and care
So for our word to be heard we must fight our cause
To stand on the world's stage and recite regardless of applause
Ah when they boo and hiss and all is amiss like paper on fire flees the bliss
So I must become a promoter a P.T. Barnum in expertise
In manic depression I fall in agony down upon my knees
Is the depression drawing me down or the mania claiming a crown?
Or do they coexist?
The twist
For in humility one does not like to carry the sign
"I am great, let us celebrate all this is mine"
Still the silent mouse is never at ease and will get no cheese
So into marketing I direct the energies of my brain
I who am one to whom the very concept of money is insane
I wish I could have rode the plains with Crazy Horse
Thousands of years before the pale man polluted the sacred source
But I am thrust into all or bust and fight I must
For if I surrender or wait upon simple chance to save the day
And so I row alone this canoe built for two up against the stream
Sylvia is wandering into a wayward whimsical dream
It seems that infinite eternity has been compressed into a single stone
And that rock has found a way into the hole of my sock
So I struggle intense as the water is full of piranhas packed so dense

Polishing the Fragments

That the stream is but one solid field of silver glowing in the sunshine
Still I am confident as night follows day that I will eventually say victory is mine
But in the glory of battle how the stratagem does insist
The twist
For artists and poets were made to be devoted to their craft
But they take our roses and conform them into a thorny crown
See the god of reality, pay for play, we insist that you bow down
As my psyche reels, do you know how eating a synthetic apple feels?
I am promised fruit if I join the greater heights of the institute
But there are rules and the ticket has a price none willingly give
How to talk, how to walk, minute scrutiny on how to live
Do not challenge the powers that be, not openly
Dissent will prevent you from reaching the atmosphere
But if you still meet success you will be co-opted have no fear
Friends and enemies they are separate which one is your list?
The twist

A World Of Giving

In the army it is a matter of pride that they don't abandon a comrade
Until they graduate from the killing machine and are left
To meander the streets and frequent homeless shelters
To battle cold, cockroaches, crazies and common cruelty
Meanwhile Wall Street wizards cast spells of scorn
When a "hero" returns in a flag draped casket they do not mourn
Business is business after all
But never do the elite answer Uncle Sam's sweet call
So there is a divide between the rich and the poor
One provokes conflicts the other is fodder for the war
This antagonism, this schism is far from conducive to living
If only we could care and share, to have a world of giving
The priority of society should be the common welfare
Profits for selfish purposes are poison in the vein
The whole damn country is clinically insane
If only we had a communal existence by cultural bonds
Brothers and sisters we could embrace and lean upon
Instead I am alone with Sylvia tending her every need
Ah but if I had the green papers to satisfy some agency's greed
I could hire the best and I could perchance get a little rest
Our devastation comes from the fixation of being supreme
That my friend is the ultimate end of the American dream
MAKE IT RICH, MAKE IT RICH, MAKE IT RICH
Money is the goal for which you forfeit the soul
Nature pristine is violently raped in a manner most obscene
We bleed to feed our selfish need as the dollar sign blinds
With obscure vision our collective decision is skewed
Utopia is possible if only we will come together
A world of giving can't you see it would be so much the better
I walk down avenues singing the blues I see a man
Huddled in a dingy green jacket a paper cup in his

Polishing the Fragments

    extended hand
A sign on brown cardboard paper is scribbled in black ink
"Homeless Veteran, Please Help"
The stink of booze compels me to seriously think
He went to some country to deliver a double dose of hell
And now "America's best" is sadly not doing so well
As masses of people march on by not even turning an eye
A few sparse straws perplexed shed a tear and wonder why
The truth that they hide from the youth
Is that the entire system is founded on a well-designed lie
The American flag upon which we boast and brag
Is but a cloth colored red, white and blue
Sad as it is that statement is true

John Kaniecki

A Lecture In Life

I was sitting in a lecture hall and my mind thought of Steven's Tech
Professor Steinman and chemistry 101
All that was missing was the gigantic chalkboards and dusty equations
That was over thirty years ago when I was young and thin
Today it was at Union County College for a crash course in dementia
Sylvia was dropped off by Vivian for the night
I finally got an extremely rare night of uninterrupted sleep
Like a rainy day in the desert
I was sitting next to Downtown Ken Brown
I gave him the nickname; that is part of my mission
Never to reign in power, perpetually the kingmaker
The speaker is a geriatric doctor, the first time I heard that term
Dementia is a disease like chewing gum on the bottom of shoes
All these sticky chemicals blocking normal thoughts
That's why Sylvia asks me the same question repeatedly
I found out that in the United States an estimated five million victims
Of this terrible form of disease are out there
Magnify that impact by considering family and friends
The agony of the illness I suppose never ends
Even death will not finish the ordeal as memories will linger
After the doctor a lawyer came up and talked
All these complications regarding mammon's manifestation: money
The government won't help with Medicaid until you are destitute
Wave the American flag as the weapons roll by, see if I salute
Afterwards Ken and I ate at the Westfield diner
The waiter was terrible but we had low expectations
Cold rolls, soda ordered without ice delivered of course with ice

Polishing the Fragments

We Americans are a spoiled lot are we not?
The misery of utter poverty is a lesson never learned thus
    never forgot
I tipped the waiter a little under fifteen percent
Not out of spite but because I always like to have a simple
    amount
So we're off back to the church building where we met
    in the morning
We talk about things, Ken and I always have a lot to talk
    about
I call Jareesa who is with Sylvia as Vivian had a meeting
I am about to go when Ken's car refuses to start
I am very reluctant to leave but Jareesa is pressed for time
I pick up Sylvia and text Ken to see if A.A.A. has come
"Do you want me to come back?" I send a text
I head back just in case, in error I make a wrong turn
Ken texts and says he is fine, he is not alone
Fortunately the women have a meeting at the church
Besides as minister he is used to being alone there anyway
But I am to do unto others as I would do unto myself
I know for certain I wouldn't want to have been left alone

A Long Night

For some reason Sylvia could not seem to rest last night
To calm my ever-increasing anger it was a fight
Ah the teapot was bursting with boiling water none thirsting for tea
I have forsaken employment to take the caregiver position
When I promised "for better or worse" I had made the decision
She leaves her room and walks out into the living room
I say go back, but she just doesn't understand
I think about the sinister seriousness of the sickness, the devil be damned
I have to focus on the struggle that God is in control
That He won't give me more heartache than I can handle
That at the end of this journey He will turn me into something better
So I count it all joy as I try to pull myself together
I have to remember that physically in the brain things just ain't right
The result is a long night
Now she is sleeping in the bedroom peaceful as a calm cool fall day
I feel the exhaustion gravitating in the back of my psyche
But I'm on a mellow ride hoping that the mania isn't manifesting in me
I am always a few pills shy of a trip to the psychiatric hospital
In truth my mind is the comparable state to a physical cripple
Like FDR playing guitar I got myself a psychedelic new deal
This is navigating a field of magic mushrooms forsaking what is real
Tripping and skipping out of reality was a remedy for escape
It captivates the mind, seduces it and then commits a brutal rape
I remember that night we dropped the mescaline pill on the colored rug

Polishing the Fragments

I searched for the capsule as if it were some hidden treasure for which I dug
Tomorrow is eternal; it is a perpetual day where God's children will say
We had one hell of a fight and man it sure was a long night
I will walk with Sylvia on those streets of gold as the promises have told
Forever young in an existence where ancient is not considered old
But for the moment I need to walk her to Jordan's shore
To complete the long goodbye, give a good cry and then no more
When you're young and the song hasn't been sung life is a delight
You aren't even aware of the truth out there and that things ain't right
And then you understand the realities of night and day
In confusion convoluted with illusion we are forced to decide upon a way
Suffering is like the wind it will blow into everyone's life frequently
Sometimes a finger prick sometimes a frontal lobotomy of agony
I recall Jesus on the cross being crucified between a pair of thieves
And this fate will recreate for every child of God who truly believes
For in refusal to surrender to the suffering and pain
If one endures it ensures that life will not have passed on planet Earth in vain
For truly to just help one wayward soul brings God great delight
So I grin and bear the sin of another long night

John Kaniecki

Rock And Roll And Rock

For a white male who in fact is not white but correctly pale
In the context of the disrespect that society places on the middle class
Where the poor are sent to war and the rich teen is given a pass
Where Vietnam was fought in the collective mind of America
Rock and Roll is the natural evolution of the sacred Constitution
Except that the indigenous peoples are not merciless and far from savage
Ask Neil Young when you are fasting drinking only water and eating cabbage
So we explore the door to the domain of the teenage brain
Where indoctrination to the ways of this nation scream contradiction
As history books are in fact highly sophisticated and hated Texas fiction
Give me five minutes of electric guitar and a cool dude defining who you are
Metal heads rode down a crazy train while I eventually went insane
Even then in the depths of dorm sixty-two and Greystone U
I was listening to the Traveling Wilburys with tweeter and the monkey man
Defining me as the sliver of self I was refining in the intricacy of God's plan
"We're not gonna take it" was a simple decree
As off went my hated classmates to go and earn the coveted degree
So they could pursue life and in the process earn the living
And thus the sellout and surrender that will never be forgiving
For what we so much hated has become replicated in I
It is something we mention in reflection that we do not deny
But personally every year my radicalization is on the

increase
I am a hippie out of time seeking to mainline pacifistic peace
Far from a rock star I am a poet with little weight behind my name
But I am throwing the dice, taking good advice, playing the game
And so you shall see that for me there is a lot more than a home by the sea
I will do my best and not rest until there is total victory
I do not have a master plan I cannot dictate the evil of the state
But I have a solution which is not found in fictional evolution
Love and peace putting it in action with direct compassion
And I am after all not another brick in the wall
Rather I stand tall totally unreal as a savage wrecking ball
I will destroy society it is a priority and all the ashes we will cart away
And the red man shall rise before Mother Earth's eyes to a grand day
Hear it I am flesh but then again women and men I Am a Spirit
Reduce it to vanity or excuse it as lunatic insanity
As all my Facebook friends sadly pretend that all is well
For I recall it all: what is seen from the teen the conflicting living hell
They have just lost innocent wisdom and sold out to the infernal system
If only they had listened to the piper singing at the gate of dawn
But alas all must pass and yesterday it is truly gone
Until the time capsule is opened by a history lover only to discover
What once was in complete control
Rock and Roll

John Kaniecki

The Heart Of The Artist

It saddens my heart like a sinking stone to know others who have grown
To a cackling warlock wishing wickedness of well-meaning folk
I am a man in a typhoon downpour while others are lapping up morning mist
I am righteous in my truth as steadfast as a redwood so I insist
For in celebration of the creation lies the heart of the artist
For when belief is a chant of spiritual relief one has the strength to resist
Hear the beating as the crashing of the waves knowing so many are slaves
I hear the thunder of the sonic boom, soon falls the doom filling the graves
Meanwhile Uncle Sam in a grand scam insists everyone behaves
Hollywood has converted and perverted the talented
Meanwhile the musical genius lives in the shelter vastly underfed
It is all a matter to shatter the resistance, certain things best unsaid
But the blood flows and the mind knows right from wrong
So in harmony that trembles the universe I sing the verse of the song
A warm welcome of we shall overcome hoping all will belong
But the masters who sit in lofty creations of concrete and glass
Sit in derision at those with vision hoping that they will swiftly pass
And one who could "imagine" a brighter world was shot down
On orders of the beast who pulls the string of the puppet with a crown
His blood gushing from the wound inflicted from one dead too soon
Understand that none of us live inside of a vacuum

Polishing the Fragments

Madmen exist and psychologists twist the darkness like stirring soup
Anger and hatred come to the top and they are encouraged not to stop
A true revolutionary always crosses the avenue with utmost caution
Paranoia strikes like a homerun hitter in batting practice
In our defense allow the public defender to announce it makes perfect sense
For those who eerily lust for power will offer any expense
Save for their own selfish self
Darwin the author of sin came up with a theory of survival of the fittest
And on the chopping block lies the heart of the artist
Who needs beauty when duty calls?
Still thump, thump, thump the exiled heart beats exposed to the air
Only in creativity can we expect to have the answer of our prayer
For oil tycoons are truly baboons who have devolved
All we need to do is rid the world of money, problem solved
But we worship the paper that is colored green
They say that every soul has some kind of price
I would challenge this and say it is some whimsical advice
While correct on the first inspect there are many who detest
Who possess the heart of the artist
Paint the picture of Jesus on the cross between two thieves crucified
And allow me now to pen poems whose accuracy cannot be denied

John Kaniecki

Red Blue Green And Of Course Invisible

Venom of a King Cobra hissing in heat at his hated fellow
Red is for the brute Blue is for the institute
Green the least obscene isn't even shown on the screen
While this Earth is temporal I put my faith in the invisible
I am wearing the colors of our flag with glaring words declaring
"I Voted Today"
Of course high-tech hackers may like hijackers take control
One more reason to vote for the invisible
After all the interference America played in coup after coup
It would be karma if somebody urinated into our cup of soup
If this is too close, red will win in sin, the color filling our street
Be optimistic either way a great evil will suffer a stunning defeat
It looks like Florida is the key which will unlock the door of doom
A belligerent finger on the button, boom, boom, boom
What's wrong with nuking a country besides twenty million slain?
Ah for the overwhelming green I can feel your pain
Bernie would have defeated both of them together, ain't that insane?
I'm already for impeachment unless of course the winner is Stein
But remember the invisible it is simply divine
Now when a child says he wants to grow up to be president
It is a sadistic lament of which we resent
We have always been a cruel nation
Genocide the foundation
Friendly utopians wearing massive grins became the Pilgrims' salvation
Then as the red man learned the tables turned towards devastation

Polishing the Fragments

Lazy lot of cretins they brought in stolen Africans
Praise the Lord here is your rewards, chains, rape and no escape
Unless of course you count the reward of heaven on high
But no relief, not a drop of comfort, until the day you die
And from Earth to Heaven came an anguished cry
Save your soul trust the invisible He is in total control
So in the land of cotton it was forgotten the serene green
On the television the map is lit up red and blue
I am certain that neither candidate truly cares about you
Its money honey and this funny game is a hysterical shame
A dust cloud full of participants proud where everything stays the same
The powerful clutch more of their desire favoring a false fame
The drama drives the drum of dreaded disaster
Down the Highway to Hell zooming ever the faster
Bigoted racism channeling a schism against the will of a Wall Street shill
And silence, none of the defiance of our green Champion Jill
But ultimately and honestly it is the will of the invisible

John Kaniecki

TIME

Sometimes tears simply roll like a creek after rain
There is no motivation, no reason to explain
Sadness over Sylvia sourly sickens my soul
Her mind has been left behind with a child to find
I powerless to help I can only aid her in her wounded state
Like a bird with a broken wing coveting once more to fly
But every day I face the reality that she will die
And that I too am mortal and shall face a similar fate
Time is the most precious commodity in this time upon Earth
If you spend your moments in Love you will get all life is worth
Silence
There are not adequate expressions even for a wordsmith
Metaphors and similes are counterfeit currency
Your wallet is stacked with green bills but none of them are acceptable money
Answers only bring deeper mysteries as you sink further in the quagmire
But there is a raging flame without a name burning in furious fire
But I am helpless to give assistance despite overwhelming desire
Sylvia is drowning in the raging water and alas I cannot swim
The best I can do is toss into the rapids some fallen tree limb
As I watch her head go under the water time after time
Wondering why this cruel sentence, what was her crime
But humanity is flawed created by God built in with sin
It is proclaimed "The wages of sin are death"
Soon I anticipate Sylvia's final, futile breath
There is more to the story a home in glory we accept it by faith
It brings hope and helps me cope but today's treacheries I must navigate
Time
Even more than the sweetest rhyme

Polishing the Fragments

Tomorrow is the promise, the gentleness of a lover's provocative kiss
I with deepest devotion shall immerse myself in the endless ocean
Eternity an irrefutable notion
Wave after wave after wave after wave after wave after wave…

Working Hard

Tick tack the clickity clack of the typewriter keys
Life is a cosmic grind that will find the best of us on our knees
One cannot walk through the meadows of eternity perpetually on guard
When you want to sing blues remember pay your dues and work hard
Cause they say if you hope and pray that Almighty God has your back
And with His divine hand He'll help you understand and provide what you lack
But you can't take promises and cash them in at the local bank
So you put the left foot in front of the right and dream with all your might
All the while you do your best to smile and of course work hard
Maybe these words of simple complexity are gibberish futility
I ponder my skills and doubt everything especially my ability
But this I know and I'll tell you so I followed my heart not my wallet
So when scrutiny of Judgment Day comes my way I'll call it
Innocent of all charges by the means of grace and mercy
Oh dear sweet Jesus please don't desert me
There is a voice the singing of a bird that cannot be heard
But through the call I hear it all the clear distinct word
So I ramble and take a gamble that somewhere you'll see this shard
I stay up late to rise early cause despite my flaws I'm working hard
Digging ditches while my mind itches as flashing fingers twitching
Chance and circumstance they dance in the sweetest romance
You charge up the hill with all your will straining to

Polishing the Fragments

    advance
But the money supply dwindles and marketing seems a great swindle
Here let me exploit you cause you ain't got a clue of what to do
I detest money but ain't it funny it is the exact thing that I desire
Sylvia needs aid and unless the help gets paid they work for one day
I refuse to surrender so I render words such as these
With quivering fingers life lingers and there ain't no easy way out
With clouds of sickening thunder one has to wonder in grave doubt
Lightning strikes, but yikes, I yearn for what burns as it turns me as a top
This sickening serenade an endless crusade my toll I've paid please stop
And the demons snicker and hope my demise will be realized quicker
And let me take a moment to say that Leonard Cohen died today
I am sad but still I'm glad that we all know that everybody goes that way
I will not finish the art he gave a start instead I will work until my hands bleed
At the moment I am not motivated by a lust of boundless greed
But rather the simplistic singularity called hoping to succeed
Though I am rather fat eating is where it's at and I like to feed my empty belly
And showering in subways stations ain't salvation and it leaves one smelly
But I'll increase the odds as I curse the gods and labor with all my might
Until the day when I say to Bob Dylan you're good but far from a delight
Vision is a gift we share and I must say that if you care you won't be conceited
When ego is immense it makes no sense and before you begin you are defeated
And so the effort of the hour has lost power and the poem is completed

John Kaniecki

STRESS

Leaf by leaf piles upon and there is no relief
Like a gazelle feeling the living hell of the scent of a lion
It is not there but he is aware it lurks within the horizon
Paranoia is lighter fluid feeding the fires of fear
Are they looking at me? An enemy is constantly near
Delusion in a nuclear inferno radiating the inner mind
Schizophrenic sadistic threats from all of the powers that be
See on the radio there is a secret code and they are talking about me
I can see in that man he got a plan don't believe his lies he's the devil in disguise
And all the while calm and tranquil the leaves accumulate
The boat will sink and if you think that you are one who is immune
I suggest you resist your pompous boasting and sing a sympathetic tune
For dementia infests an estimated five million in the United States
But there are no answers or even mentions in political debates
Instead they promise to build a wall or devise war plans to end it all
What do I care about a nuclear nightmare when Sylvia slips?
Down an endless slide she takes the ride and I have no place to hide
I look to the Lord above in tender love and pray I can cope
That I may overcome and not succumb to poverty that is my hope
Some men want to be king others accumulate endless supplies of money
I just want all to be well so my soul I won't have to sell to support my honey
And I who should be at rest am facing a test that is challenging to the best
A dementia caregiver is said to work the thirty-six hour day all without pay
The savings plunge as the demon stress lunges with red-

hot claws glowing
I seek a miracle something wonderful that is almost impossible while knowing
God is able
So I sit writing poems and creating books that don't sell investing in a fable
But it is my prayer that with tender care God divine will smile and His face will shine
Illuminating the treacherous path so I can avoid pitfalls and in the aftermath
As I turn to what I did transverse I can say how He led me to blessing from curse
All the while I smile knowing that the masses have things so much worse
I am warm and well-fed even with a bed upon which I can lay down my head
Still it will be a sorrowful surrender when I buy Sylvia a ticket one way
To head home to Grenada for some peace and to live her last day
I refuse to subjugate Sylvia to torment for a nursing home to be put in
Where they let you sit stinking in your feces and urine
Money in this world it truly cannot buy you love or anything near
But bloodsuckers and midnight truckers will magically appear
When the green bills are flaunted all the while I am haunted
Knowing that if mankind is to keep growing money must be eliminated
So in my brain that went insane I desire something sorely hated
Jesus said, "If you seek to be perfect sell all you have and give it to the poor"
I obeyed one day and they locked me up, I was free no more
To each their own I guess, stress

Death And After Life

All good people go to heaven and especially good dogs
Not the mean snarling junkyard dog on the rusty chain however
But the cute ones in the dog food commercials they are so clever
And so Peter's wife tragically dies in the midst of my madness
I write a poem trite depicting a reunification in sweet salvation
Wading in the waters of heaven shore still together as before
Am I a hypocrite, full of it, a professional liar?
Should I sing and sting with an ominous threat of hellfire?
Of course eternal life is open only to those of my narrow sect
Why who else in the whole wide world would God respect?
But there is something about Truth with a capital T
That reality is subject to an absolute technicality
Either up is down or down is up either way will it fill your cup?
People who disrespect and neglect the Almighty in His power
Until the sudden realization that now is the final hour
Ah to find a brave man when they stare into the face of death
Who will kiss the reaper and embrace that chilly breath
Of course atheists insist that He is just an imaginary friend
Something that helps us cope and brings hope in the bitter end
But Love that is the deity defined in the divine person of Jesus
Not the Jesus of the mercenaries who have ravaged the Earth
It takes more to make a Christian than belief in the virgin birth
You have to Love everybody that ultimately is what will prove your worth
And on judgment day the Lord with his standards shall measure your girth

Polishing the Fragments

Kindness, compassion, generosity, faith, and above all the call of Love
And yes one billion Chinese can all be wrong
It's like having the wrong melody and trying to fit it into a song
Trying to place the square peg into a five dimensional hole
Only God can create a universe and only God can give life to a soul
You see with certainty that a man does not live until they give God control
A born-again moment where they repent and accept the message sent
But for Peter I wrote words, like a shot of Vodka to ease the pain
A shimmering ray of sunshine in a today tormented by endless rain
I whistle a merry tune in the month of June for soon the devourer will consume
Apocalypse slips into the frontal lobe and all around the globe doom
As armies march to war Babylon the Whore hisses to deplore
Our American state full of hate is immersed into a brutal bloody debate
Refugees in anguished pleas learn the inhuman lesson of oppression
And I am most depressed that Peter was not blessed with a long marriage
And he was another of those who claimed friendship only to abandon me
In the throes of my madness, deplored and ignored in my insanity
So I throw a bone to the Great Stantone sorry he is now all alone
He is not here but I fear that loud and clear there is a miserable moan
And so to his wife in poetic verse I offer hope of eternal life

A Flash

Some poetry is pretty some poetry is in disguise but actually prose
This work of art well it ain't neither of those
I am the pale face prophet singing salvation on a desolate corner in the hood
I am on Wall Street with a tin cup and a sign saying "support the better good"
I am standing against pipelines and money in general
I am declaring that the greatest thinker of our generation is John Africa
But before I could let my brain function I had to have the crash
All those systematic defenses built in to exclude sin
Well they fell to hell in a flash
Except the white righteous virtue that was purer than snow
Well I cannot pretend that it was anything but yellow
America it never lost in a war, I was taught that and so much more
We are the land of the free which treats all equally
Blacks three fifths a person
Indians merciless savages
Women no vote
If the poor didn't have guns we never would have gotten the Bill of Rights
So much truth excluded, the books full of distortions and outright lies
"Manifest Destiny" is the malevolent anguish of cries
On the dollar bill "In God We Trust" it refers to Baal
While in the name of eugenics abortions are truly sacrifices to sexual promiscuity
Making it personal between Catholicism and patriotism I was a robot
It took me years to unlearn what I should have forgot
God the great I Am was really Uncle Sam sitting on his shining white throne
Money was the key to happiness and subtle compassions were best unknown
And if I was to step out of line God divine would strike

from the blue with a lightning
FLASH!!!
I found more truth in smoking marijuana and I wish I tried some hash
Life is a race of disgrace and everybody is off running in a mad futile dash
I need to mention that humanity is running in the wrong direction
So many racing down the Freeway where the cars are shooting stars
Still to this day my body, my mind, my spirit it carries the scars
But my soul beyond the fantastical dream is pure and clean
I am Frankenstein, a monster hewed together of sown body parts
Satan is a master but he has only stolen the secrets of the arts
Light is a delight full of might that will make everything right
We simply have to persevere through torment and fear is that clear?
I see an army of misinformed hypocrites marching with poster signs
"I am Jesus' right-hand man" the diabolical designs
Never stopping and dropping down to a place of grace in submission
When your fragmented and tormented ego is summarily prevented

John Kaniecki

My Eulogy

"At least he tried"
Those words alone engraved on my tombstone
Mother she would have cried
And father denied, any wrongdoing
A storm to conform is brewing
Fascists dress in similar uniform
Take heed as I warn

I am a broken man
Perhaps it was God's plan
They crushed me into fragments
But the Almighty with delicate hand
Polished every last piece
And understand
In the final release
He shall cast my broken bones high
Into the midnight darkness of the sky
And my fragments shall radiate
A testimony against cruelty and hate
And there across the universe
For better or worse
Shall be the remnants of my mind
And if some lost soul shall find
That they are lost in this wayward world
I pray that they could look above
And be reminded that all is Love
That is what I wish to impart
The message upon my heart
To you from me

    In all simplicity
The stars of the night
My scars of the fight
May they give you some light
Sylvia please don't cry
Goodbye

About the Author

John Kaniecki is a poet and prose writer residing with his wife Sylvia in lovely Montclair, New Jersey. John currently has nine books out, five of poetry and four of prose with more to come. John's primary function is as a caregiver to his wife Sylvia. John also is an activist as a member of Woman's International League Of Peace And Freedom as well as New Jersey Peace Action. John is a minister of the Church Of Christ At Chancellor Avenue which is located in the South Ward of Newark. John has suffered from bipolar disorder since that age of twenty. His story is told in his memoirs "More Than The Madness" also published by Dreaming Big Publications.

Made in the USA
Lexington, KY
11 December 2019